MW01178766

SPIRITUALITY:
Inner Armor

Jim Amsing

 FriesenPress

Suite 300 - 990 Fort St
Victoria, BC, V8V 3K2
Canada

www.friesenpress.com

Copyright © 2019 by Jim Amsing
First Edition — 2019

All rights reserved.

No part of this publication may be reproduced in any form, or by any
means, electronic or mechanical, including photocopying, recording, or any
information browsing, storage, or retrieval system, without permission in
writing from FriesenPress.

ISBN
978-1-5255-4889-5 (Hardcover)
978-1-5255-4890-1 (Paperback)
978-1-5255-4891-8 (eBook)

1. SELF-HELP, SPIRITUAL

Distributed to the trade by The Ingram Book Company

CONTENTS

INTRODUCTION

Dedicated to those who have paid the ultimate price of
selfless service.

We are not humans having a spiritual experience.
We are spiritual beings having a human experience.

Pierre Teilhard de Chardin

The consequence for not adequately training your Huns
is their failure to accomplish that which is expected of them.

Wess Roberts, PhD, *Leadership Secrets of Attila the Hun*

What defines a SEAL is his unwillingness to ever, ever give up. It
requires extraordinary will in all three aspects of human existence:
body, mind and spirit. Very, very few men are dominant in all three.

Scott McEwen and Richard Miniter in, *Eyes on Target*

To combat the diabolical schemes and toxic complexities of
criminal evil (e.g., violence, terrorism, and gangs) during the
twenty-first century, officers must constantly revitalize and
safeguard their inner spirituality.

Special Agent Samuel L. Feemster, FBI Behavioral Science
Unit in *Wellness and Spirituality: Beyond Survival Practices for*
Wounded Warriors

AUTHOR'S NOTE

The stories in this book are true and the author deeply
appreciates the officers who contributed their experiences.
Names have been changed for privacy. Named locations
have been changed because these stories, or versions
thereof, could happen anywhere.

~

PROLOGUE

Vanessa was terrified, and the cocaine hadn't helped the situation. Jared, her pimp, had put a shotgun to her head and threatened to blow it off if she didn't turn more tricks.

She felt trapped and desperate. When Jared grabbed Gina and took her into the other room, Vanessa ran out of the front door as fast as she could. She couldn't help screaming as she ran along 9th Ave. She couldn't take it anymore. Why did men have to be such pigs?

Officer Bruce Torrey responded to the call of a screaming, half-naked female running down 9th Ave. It sounded like the most interesting call of the night so far. He found her on 9th Ave., gasping and sweating from running down the middle of the street and heard her say repeatedly that some black guys were trying to kill her with shotguns.

She wouldn't tell the police her name, and she appeared to be in a drug-induced frenzy.

To Bruce she looked like a hooker. She was an attractive black woman wearing a skimpy halter-top and shorts. Most prostitutes looked quite hardened after a few years working the streets, but she looked frightened and confused.

Thank God the paramedics showed up and took her to General Hospital. Bruce chalked it up to a sad situation, and would have liked to talk to her further, but she was incoherent.

Three days later he was on day shift and decided to do some radar speed checks on 9th Ave. It was good pickings in the area as people loved to zoom out of the downtown core to get home.

The same attractive hooker came to his window and thanked him for helping her. Bruce wondered how she even recognized him as she had seemed totally out of it the other night.

"My pimp and his pal had really pointed their shotguns at me when I was running here the other night!"

Bruce asked her if she wanted to talk and she seemed grateful for a listening ear. The usual story of an unwed mother and no father at home emerged. To Bruce it seemed that in this case there was a willingness in Vanessa to actually make a change in her life.

"Vanessa, do you want to get off the street and get your life back?"

She thought for a few moments and then said, "Officer, I want to get away from these men, and this life, but I've got nowhere to go."

Bruce marveled at the timing. He had just been introduced to Sister Bernadette, who ran a ministry called Servant Anonymous. It provided a safe house for those escaping from prostitution, as well as helping the women beat their drug addictions. They moved the girls from the big city into a small town, and also provided vocational training that would allow them to get real jobs.

"Would you be willing to go to a safe house for women getting out of prostitution right now? I spoke to Sister Bernadette at Servant Anonymous just this week, and they have a safe place for you to stay. What do you say?"

Vanessa looked intently at the officer to see if there was any deceit and saw only compassion and concern and decided to take the chance on making the change, and didn't even get any of her clothes or other belongings.

Bruce reflected on how incredible it felt to be privileged to help Vanessa. He hoped and prayed that her courage would persevere into a new life.

INTRODUCTION

Most persons involved in the field of law enforcement and peace keeping hope that their personal and professional lives will somehow survive the toxic effects of dealing with evil.

What many officers don't realize is that an informed moral conscience infused with spiritual wisdom and virtues, will transform despair and cynicism into a daily rhythm of life-changing opportunities to assist and protect those they have sworn to serve.

We all have a choice to develop a spirituality that taps into the healing power of service for those we love, and those we have been chosen to serve. This energy, when harnessed and integrated within the inner person, will necessarily be reflected in the actions of the outer person.

When we are willing to be a conduit for peace keeping, our sixth sense; our intuition, our ability to know what the right investigative avenue or tactical decision should be, allows us to serve in a way that moves us beyond the rational and into the mystical field of spirituality.

Courage under fire or dignity in the face of criticism for doing the right thing is framed internally within the context of a desire to work for the good, despite challenges from within and without. This type of spirituality allows us to push past the barriers of fear that hinder so many in the quest for peace, justice, and mercy. Marcus Aurelius said, "He who lives in harmony with himself lives in harmony with the universe."

Protecting the vulnerable of society from the predators bestows a sacred trust and honorable vocation to those chosen, equipped, and willing to serve. This sacred trust that society gives to its peace officers is corroded every time an officer fails to live up to the exacting demands of integrity, honesty, fairness, and courage. When cynicism, apathy, narcissism, arrogance, hatred, and despair cloud and darken our attitude and demeanor toward those we serve, it drives a wedge of hostility and distrust into every interaction.

Sir Robert Peel, the acknowledged English leader of modern policing, stated that without the consent of the people, policing was impossible.

What is the alternative to the current slide of public trust?

Every time an act of peace is performed it builds society's fabric. When a humble, polite, and respectful tone and action can be used it should be. Courageous, life-saving actions or hope enabled build trust. When going above and beyond the call of duty is the norm for you, with a willingness to lend a helping hand, you build society. Finding solutions and connecting people to social, mental, and spiritual resources become a road towards hope and create changes in attitudes as well as circumstances.

I protest, you say! How can you say I'm not doing my job properly if I'm a bit cynical because of exposure to man's inhumanity to man? Look at the fallout of thefts, assaults, rapes, child abuse, murder, robbery, horrendous accidents and the like, and their impact on victims and those investigating the crimes.

Not only that, but look at what causes the stress to police officers; petty and vindictive citizen complaints; bullying and arrogant supervisors; courts that emphasize legality over justice. How is one to maneuver through the minefield of physical, mental, and spiritual hurdles to survive this type of profession?

Most police services provide decent physical and mental preparation and training, but few departments prepare their officers for the toxic effects policing has on their spiritual psyches. Mind, body, and spirit need to be in balance for a police officer to operate effectively on and off the job.

Resiliency against temptations, trials, and trauma begins in the inner person. When we are in balance in our physical, mental, and spiritual spheres we can serve others out of interior harmony and peace.

The downturn in public trust, the divorce rate in policing, and destroyed lives from substance abuse and suicide are all indicators of a profession in trouble.

Spiritual training at all stages of a career will help mitigate the huge cost of staff turnover, stress and medical leave, suicide, and relationship issues. It would help in generating a return to the public service Sir Robert Peel envisioned; "The police are the public and the public are the police; the police being only members of the public who are paid to give full-time attention to duties which are incumbent on every citizen in the interests of community welfare and existence."

I have over twenty-five years of experience in the law-enforcement field in big city and small-town policing, as well as serving as a police chaplain in a major city for thirteen years. Spirituality has been one of the main factors for longevity in my marriage and family life, as well as the means to thrive in a toxic policing environment. Although my personal spirituality is rooted in a Christian heritage, wisdom from spiritual and moral masters of different traditions, along with true-life police stories will help to ground the theory that when we tap into our spiritual genius, the power of transforming lives, including our own, will astound, encourage, and motivate us to be game-changers in the modern world.

This book will also look at the Diakonos Peace Officer Retreat Society, which is now called the Legacy Place Society. This organization was formed to address the educational, spiritual, and physical gaps in meeting the needs of emergency-service members and families, as well as to face the challenges of forging a new path through the forest of resistance to change.

I hope that we can be a piece of the puzzle of life for each other and continue to learn and grow as we share our experiences—that you will reflect on the values you're willing to live and die for. I will ask you to review the reasons you swore an oath to serve and protect, and be willing to face the truth. *What are my virtues and vices, and do I want to do anything about them? Can I achieve Abraham Maslow's self-actualization if I embrace a willingness to learn universal wisdom through study and implementation of spirituality into my inner being?*

Peacemaking is a state of mind and of the heart. When you put on your outer armor for protection you shouldn't forget that spirituality is a dynamic inner-armor that will protect your soul, guide you in peril, and allow you to live without fear.

You can *tap into* the powerful flow of spirituality through an on-going willingness to be renewed, changed, and challenged. Be prepared for the ride of your life.

CHAPTER 1

Overcome Evil with Good—
Bono Malum Superate

~Life is neither good or evil but only a place for good and evil.

Marcus Aurelius~

Officer Joe Adams put on his body armor. Sue, his wife, had made him promise early in his career to put it on for every shift. At times in the summer it was tempting not to wear it because of the heat, but he had given his word. She had reminded him that the kids needed a father who was there for them and that she wanted a husband to grow old with.

Not a bad sentiment, at that. Lots of police marriages broke up, but he was one of the lucky ones with over twenty years of marriage to his soul mate. He'd rather cut off his right arm than disappoint her.

While he buckled on his duty belt, the noise of his squad mates cracking jokes, banging lockers, and roughhousing made him smile. His partner, Officer Roy Buckley, was usually in the thick of things and liked to get a good laugh out of everyone. The evening shift promised to be fun.

Joe knew that he needed to put on his inner armor as well as his body armor. He liked to call it his spiritual armor. His guardian angel often had to work overtime for him, and it was comforting to know he had spiritual backup. He said a quick prayer for his safety as well as for that of his squad-mates, and off it was to the fun and games with his partner Roy.

Officer Roy Buckley knew that Joe wore a St. Michael, the Archangel, medallion around his neck and figured it was okay. Every little bit helped on the street and you really didn't know what you'd run into.

Roy was driving, as usual, and they hit the streets looking for action. One of the first calls of the night was at the Blue Lagoon Tavern and Hotel.

The seedy hotel, on the edge of the downtown core, flashed blue neon lights as the officers pulled up front for a disturbance in the downstairs bar.

Inside the bar, Roy grabbed one of the two drunks fighting and Joe grabbed the other. Roy asked his guy, "Hey, what are you fighting for?"

The man replied that his former friend, Terry, had muscled in on his girlfriend and that he was standing up for her.

Terry looked disgusted and replied, "She's not your girlfriend, stupid! She's a hooker and is everyone's girlfriend...if you have the money."

The two drunks tried to get at each other again but were firmly held by Roy and Joe.

"Okay, Roy," said Joe. "Let's get these guys' names, addresses and D.O.B.s. Maybe we'll get lucky and they'll have some warrants."

When the check for warrants came up negative, the two ex-friends decided they were buddies again and asked if they could go back to the bar for more beers. Joe and Roy exchanged a knowing look and warned them to stay out of trouble, or they would both go to the lockup together.

An hour later, the officers got an interesting call. A First Nations prostitute had escaped from a basement prison where she and another gal were being forced to service Arab-looking men waiting their turn in an upstairs pizza parlor. The girls had been drugged and kept locked in a basement room behind a plywood door, which was locked on the outside. The escaped girl had vaguely described the area as just south of the downtown core on a major roadway.

Roy and Joe found the Shawarma and Two-for-One Pizza Parlor in the general area described and noticed about ten Lebanese males hanging about. When the police approached them, all the men got very nervous and looked like they wanted to bolt. Joe and Roy called for backup to get ID off these guys. None of the ten were willing to volunteer what he was doing in the pizza parlor. No pizzas looked to be baking in the ovens.

A back door led to the alley. The business was one of a couple in a decrepit, hundred-year-old sandstone building. There was no basement access under the pizza shop, but as they walked farther down the alley Roy and Joe saw a basement stairwell.

The basement was filthy with old garbage, spider webs, and debris. At the far end was a metal shower stall with green slime all over it. A plywood door with a combination lock and door hasp on the outside was visible at the far end of the basement. A couple of half-eaten cartons of Chinese food were on the floor beside the door.

Joe kicked in the locked door and spotted a young, First Nations girl lying naked on a single, bare mattress. She appeared to be drugged.

EMS were called in to take the girl to the hospital, and the vice detectives arrived to conduct an investigation into the sex-slave trade going on in the basement. Roy figured the front page of the newspaper tomorrow would have the vice-squad commander patting himself on the back for the great work his team had done cracking the case.

Joe felt the rage build up within himself. These perverts needed to be read to from the "Good Book" and he was willing to do the teaching. The problem was, they couldn't tie these guys directly to the basement room where the girls had been held. Both of the girls, who were all of fourteen-years-old, had been drugged and couldn't ID any of the men. The men wouldn't talk, but guilt was written all over their faces.

Roy and Joe had rescued damsels in distress, but justice was denied the girls. It was galling and frustrating. The officers hit the streets again.

It quieted down substantially after two in the morning and they cruised the streets and avenues of the downtown core looking for something to do.

"Hey, Roy, let's grab a coffee. I'm fading fast."

"I'm with you on that, Joe. Where do you want to go?"

Just then Joe looked at the warehouse across the intersection. He was aware that it housed some kind of communications company, which had a parking lot on the east side of the building with a bunch of white service vans.

Joe immediately sensed that there was a dead body on the east side of the building. It wasn't an interior voice, but just a sure knowledge. He and Roy hadn't been dispatched to the location; but he just knew.

"Roy, there's a dead body on the other side of that building!"

Roy wanted to ask him how he could know that, but enough strange things had occurred while he'd been working with Joe that he didn't ask any questions.

They drove through the intersection to where the vans were in rows off an alley beside the building. When they got about two-thirds of the way down the alley Joe told Roy to stop. Between two vans he had seen a body completely hidden from the street.

It was Terry, the drunk from the Blue Lagoon. He was lying on his back with what looked like multiple stab wounds to the chest. Joe checked to see if he had a pulse, but it looked like he had been dead for a couple of hours as rigor mortis had set in. Joe called it in to dispatch and had a car crew arrest Terry's "friend," who lived at the Blue Lagoon. The car crew was to take the suspect to the detention room at police HQ to await the arrival of the homicide detectives.

Roy shook his head. They had solved a non-dispatched homicide in five minutes or less. How had Joe known the body was there? Roy wouldn't have believed it if he hadn't been there to witness it himself. Talk about police instinct, or intuition, or whatever you call it. Joe had it in spades.

It was going to be hours before the homicide dicks finished combing their hair, had breakfast, and leisurely made their way to the scene. It was going to be a long night. They would be doing continuity on this stiff for hours until they released the body to the medical examiner's morgue.

~

Mother Theresa of Calcutta asks us to see the face of Christ in everyone we meet, and yet, for police officers this can be quite a challenge. In her work with the poor she noted that, "Loneliness and the feeling of being unwanted is the most terrible poverty."

Many times for the police it feels that when you look in the face of evil the impulse is to crush it like a bug.

Police officers respond more readily to Romans 13: 3-4 NAB where sacred scriptures tell us: "For rulers are not a terror to good works, but to evil. Do you want to be unafraid of authority? Do what is good, and you will have praise from the same. For he is God's minister to you for good. But if you do evil, be afraid; for he does not bear the sword in vain; for he is God's minister, an avenger to execute wrath on him who practices evil."

The key to understanding is that those on the thin blue line keep evil at bay and protect the weak and vulnerable. They don't bear the sword in vain but use force, when needed, to protect and defend themselves, as well as those they serve.

Those who are marginalized and oppressed in society may not have any other advocate than the police.

Jesus taught that compassion for the poor, hungry, lonely, and imprisoned was the same as doing it for him because of his identity with them. "As you did it to one of the least of these my brethren, you did it to me." (Matthew 25:40 NAB)

Police officers can emulate this compassion and service and can suffer with the marginalized. A kind word and a respectful attitude can be the catalyst for hope for those they serve.

The Dalai Lama says that a healthy, compassionate motivation is the foundation of spiritual growth.[1]

St. John Chrysostom, an early Church father, taught that our Lord is not merely seeking to do away with all kinds of controversy and enmity between men, he is asking more of us; that we try to bring peace, no less, to those who hate us. [2]

Spiritual intelligence is needed to meet this challenge. Fontana describes the concept of spiritual intelligence as; the ability to be creative, to alter the boundaries of current thought... to address problems of good and evil, to exercise extended choice, to seek higher meaning in life, and to transform both the self and life situations in positive ways. [3]

Compassion is the key to achieving a deeper level of morality; yet how can we help others when we ourselves are beset by wrong attitudes? [4]

For St. Augustine, our pilgrimage on earth cannot be exempt from trial. We progress by means of trial. No one knows himself except through trial, or receives a crown except after victory, or strives except against an enemy or temptation. [5]

Police officers when faced with fear, despair, hopelessness, and loneliness are challenged to bring hope, compassion, kind-heartedness, and comfort to the people they serve.

Can they be instruments of both justice and mercy?

The level of inner armor, and the resiliency of our spirituality will answer the question of how well police officers, and others involved in service to others, overcome evil with good.

ENDNOTES:

1. Dalai Lama, *How to Practice the way to a Meaningful Life*, Translated and edited by Jeffrey Hopkins, PhD. (New York, London, Toronto, Singapore: Atria Books, 2002), p. 14.

2. Francis Fernandez, "St. John Chrysostom, Homily on Matthew 15:4, In Conversation with God." (London, New York, Nairobi, New Delhi: *Scepter*, Vol. 1, 1986), p. 21.

3. Jonathan Smith and Ginger Charles, "The relevance of spirituality in policing: a dual analysis." (*International Journal of Police Science & Management*, volume 12, Number 3), p. 323.

4. Dalai Lama, *How to Practice the way to a Meaningful Life*, p.95.

5. St. Augustine, *Commentary on Psalms*, (Ps. 60, 2-3: CCL 39, 766) Lenten and Easter Season, Liturgy Of The Hours (New York: Catholic Book Publishing Co., 1976), p.87.

CHAPTER 2

Fire Tests Gold—Ignis Aurum Probat

*~If a man has not discovered something that
he will die for, he isn't fit to live.*

Martin Luther King Jr.~

O fficer Ron Arthur was happy he was working with Don Shepherd on night shift. At six feet and 270 lbs. Don was a big man who loved to tackle bad guys that made the mistake of running and always tried to elbow him aside when a door needed to be kicked in. Ron and Don had worked together for a couple of years and knew what the other was thinking most of the time. They both shared a strong Christian faith and a spirituality that helped them through tough calls.

At 0100 hrs., police dispatch received a call from a citizen who reported seeing a male with a woman draped over his shoulder, throw the woman into a grey panel van and drive off southbound on 9th street from in front of a three-story apartment just off 12th Avenue South East. No license number on the grey van was available, and because of poor lighting a description of the two people was vague.

When Ron and Don got to the scene they saw an older, decrepit, weathered-brown three-story walk-up apartment building. The suspect vehicle was long gone and all was quiet. They decided to go into the small lobby of the apartment building to see what they could find. Inside, they heard loud noises and then a male swearing profusely from an upper floor.

As they made their way up the creaky stairs, trying to stay on the edge of the stair treads to reduce the noise, they noticed a small, round mirror on the wall of the stairwell between the second and third floors, positioned in a way that someone on the third floor could observe who was coming up the stairwell. Drug dealers used these types of mirrors and Ron and Don both continued cautiously up to the third-floor landing.

Ron sighted a man standing in the doorway of an apartment swearing a blue streak. The male was holding a twelve-inch butcher knife in his right hand and when he spotted the police, he yelled, "Kill me! Kill me!"

Ron drew his semi-automatic Glock pistol, pointed it at the male and said, "Police, drop the knife!" When the man refused to drop the knife and kept repeating over and over that he wanted them to kill him, Ron remembered from his tactical training that a man with a knife could travel twenty feet in two to three seconds. He figured that if the man came towards him with the knife he would keep putting rounds into him until the guy dropped. Although they had been taught to double tap, the reality was that in a tactical deadly-force situation you kept shooting until the threat was neutralized.

Ron heard an interior voice say, *Pepper spray him!* He didn't know if he had much pepper spray left in the bottle on his belt, as he was known as "Dr. Pepper" in the downtown division for all the times he had used pepper spray. The effective spray distance with a full bottle of pepper spray was five to eight feet, and he was at least twenty-five feet from the guy with the knife.

With his left hand he took the pepper spray from the pouch on his duty belt and tried pepper spraying the bad guy. The pepper spray must have had angel wings, because it hit the guy right between the horns. He dropped like a rock and kept yelling, "You should have killed me!"

After they had decontaminated the eyes of the bad guy, whose name they learned was Cory Orrin, they obtained information from him as to what happened that night. They found out that Cory had had a girl over that he was planning to have sex with, and then his buddy Dan Gordon and Dan's girlfriend Chrystal arrived to party. After doing a couple of lines of coke, Dan had started arguing with his girlfriend, knocked her out, slung her over his shoulder, and left. When the girl Cory had invited to the party saw this she'd left as well. Cory was upset that his "date" for the night had left.

Some further questioning led to an address for Dan in the northeast part of the city and after calling for another car crew to transport Cory to cells, away Don and Ron went to arrest the buddy for assault and kidnapping. When they got to the location they noted an older gray van in front of a run-down condo.

When Ron knocked on the front door, a muscular, thirty-five-year-old male covered in tattoos answered and said, "What?" They asked him if he was Dan Gordon, the owner of the van, and he replied, "Yeah, so what is it to you?" They announced they were arresting him and the fight was on. Dan was a seriously bad guy with an extensive record, who had an outstanding warrant for assault.

After twisting him into a pretzel and handcuffing him, they gave Dan his rights and went looking for the girlfriend. They found Chrystal in an upstairs bedroom lying naked and tied to the four corner posts of the bed. A look of terror was on her face until she recognized them as the police.

Chrystal Armstrong related that after her boyfriend Dan had knocked her out and brought her to the condo he had woken her

SPIRITUALITY: INNER ARMOUR

up with cold water and then told her he was going to kill her. He had taken her clothes off, tied her to the bed, and then showed her the knife he was going to use. She'd heard the knocking on the front door and had prayed someone would save her.

After getting a written statement from Chrystal and seizing the knife, they took Dan to jail. Another car crew took Chrystal to a friend's place for safety.

When the paperwork was done the cops went for a coffee and debriefed. They had been in a deadly-force environment and had found a way, with help, not to shoot the witness to the kidnapping and assault. If Cory Orrin had attacked with the knife he would have been shot, and they would not have been able to save Chrystal from being killed by her boyfriend, Dan.

The timing had been cute with getting to Dan's condo in time to prevent the homicide. A lot of moving pieces in the cosmic world had come together for a successful conclusion to this incident.

Both officers felt completely calm about the events that had taken place and they chalked it up to their guardian angels giving them a lot of help. Their faith told them that they were not only being protected but guided to be there for those who needed protection the most urgently.

For both of them it had been a privilege to serve and save lives. The exposure to evil and the effects of toxic stress had been greatly reduced for them because of their faith and spirituality. They were looking forward to the next adventure and opportunity that would present itself to them.

For some reason they always seemed to be in the thick of the action. They were *tapped in*. Maybe it was because they were always available and willing to answer the call.

*~A small body of determined spirits fired by an unquenchable faith
in their mission can alter the course of history.*

Mahatma Gandhi~

Peacemaking is a noble mission.

Many police officers suffer the toxic effects of evil because they haven't equipped or prepared themselves for battle with evil. As Marcus Aurelius stated, "Life is neither good or evil, but only a place for good and evil."

If we realize that everyone has free will to choose good and evil actions, we can begin to get a handle on why bad things happen to good people. It is because someone's evil actions have impinged on another person, or persons' autonomy.

As the guardians of society, police officers have a God-given and community-authorized mandate to stop evil actions, and those who precipitate them.

It's called the thin blue line for a reason. Good and evil is the choice each one of us makes every day. Police departments try to hire those persons that demonstrate the highest levels of integrity, honesty, fortitude, perseverance, and intellect that they can find in society and then train and equip them to fight the battle against evil on their behalf.

The problem is that battling evil sucks the life out of officers like a vampire. When police officers haven't been taught how to replenish their life energies properly, a breakdown occurs in the values and ethics that they brought to the job.

Maintaining a good workout regime helps to reduce stress and can keep the body healthy, but without a replenishing of the mind and spirit, the toxic effects of evil will take their toll.

Marriage and relationship breakdowns, despondency, despair, substance abuse, job attrition, and suicide are all symptoms of officers who are unable to cope with toxic stress in healthy ways.

The antidote to unnecessary breakdown because of the toxic effects of exposure to evil is a spirituality that replenishes, renews, and restores your life energy. Inner armor is a spirituality that restores balance, harmony, tranquility, joy, and peace in the inner person. Peace in the inner person equips one to be a peace-keeper in our outer world.

Blessed are we when we know how to bring peace to the afflicted; when we serve as instruments of unity in our families, among our workmates, and in all those we meet in the course of our daily lives. [1]

The Dalai Lama teaches that for whoever holds love and com-passion in high esteem, the practice of tolerance is essential, and it requires an enemy. We must be grateful to our enemies then, because they help us engender a serene mind! [2]

A serene mind in policing involves looking at our enemies as persons who have taken a wrong path by choosing evil, but who still need us to be compassionate and champions of the right path. Although many hardened criminals view compassion as a weak-ness, some may see an authenticity in our treatment of them that compels them to ask what gives us hope.

An integrated spirituality can give you the freedom to engage in a meaningful dialogue with all the members of society, good or evil.

Humility is a virtue of being authentic and without pre-tense or arrogance. [3]

Police officers who grow in wisdom, compassion, courage, and humility during their careers will be the catalyst for an engaged police department that has earned the admiration, respect, and especially the trust of the community it serves.

ENDNOTES:

1. Francis Fernandez, "In Conversation with God." (London, New York, Nairobi, New Delhi: *Scepter*, Volume 1, 1994), p.20.

2. Dalai Lama, *My Spiritual Journey*, collected by Sofia Stril-Rever (New York, NY., Paris, France: HarperOne and Presses de la Renaissance, 2009-2010), p. 28.

3. James C. Hunter, *The Servant, A Simple Story about the True Essence of Leadership* (New York: Crown Business, Random House Inc., 1998,2002), p.110.

CHAPTER 3

Ready for Anything—In Omnia Paratus

*~Just as a candle cannot burn without fire, men
cannot live without a spiritual life.*

Buddha~

The 911 call of a robbery in progress came in from Terry Cameron, the clerk at the bike shop across from the Subway sandwich shop on 4th Street. He was observing a male with a black trench-coat pointing a handgun at the female server in the shop.

Officers Conrad Turner and Dom Dimatti loved these types of adrenalin-charged calls. It sounded like a live one, as the bike clerk was still talking to the 911 dispatcher. Luckily they were only five blocks away.

For some reason, no other car crews were available for backup even though it was dayshift, and that created a problem. Conrad and Dom knew the location well. The sub shop was in a block of businesses that shared a common wall. The second floor above the businesses contained offices. The sub shop was beside the liquor store located on the corner of the block.

Normally, police would surround the business with cars to block an escape and wait for the robber to come out. Then, from the safety of their police vehicles they would tell him, or her, to put their weapon down and surrender or die. Of course, the officers would be pointing a shotgun or carbine at the robber to get their attention, but in this situation Conrad and Dom had no backup. The bad guy coming out the door would be able to see them, and then he'd deke into the adjacent liquor store and out the back door and be on his way.

The officers parked at the end of the block by the Irish pub, ran along the front of the businesses, and got tight to the front door.

Dom was going to challenge the robber as he came out the front door. The partners had never used this tactic before, but the situation demanded it.

Dom felt the adrenalin kick in. You didn't get the chance very often to catch the robber in the act, and here Dom was in tight on the doorway ready to challenge the bad guy. He had his semi-auto Glock pistol in the ready position, and it was a comfort to know Conrad had his back.

A person fitting the description of wearing a long, black trench-coat came out the front door carrying a long-barreled handgun.

"Police! Drop the weapon! Drop the weapon! Police!"

The guy in the trench-coat was only three feet away and he started to raise the weapon toward Dom. Dom knew he would have to shoot before the guy shot him, and he'd begun trigger pull, when unexpectedly he heard the interior voice that had saved his life so often say, "Reach out and touch!"

Instantly, he switched the gun to his weak hand, grabbed the robber by the trench-coat with his strong hand, and did an absolute power slam onto the sidewalk. The guy's gun went flying. Dom did a quick speed cuff, and then he raised his gun to cover the threat of any other potential robbers.

A bunch of teenagers, with what looked like a commercial-quality video camera, were staring at him in shock.

A man who identified himself as the drama teacher of the high school three blocks away, explained that they had been doing a robbery re-enactment for a high school drama production.

As Conrad chewed out the drama teacher, Dom was still vibrating from the adrenalin dump. He looked down at his handcuffed prisoner.

A frightened, pretty, sixteen-year-old girl with dark-brown hair tucked under a cap, looked up at him. She was the same age as his oldest daughter. He had come within a split second of shooting an innocent girl. For whatever reason, the teacher had failed to notify the police about the drama production.

It certainly had turned into a major drama for Dom and the young student "robber."

Dom knew he was justified in law to have taken the shot, but also knew he wouldn't have been able to justify it to himself or to the public that would have crucified him. His guardian angel had saved him from taking a life. It wasn't the first time Dom had gotten *life-changing* and *life-saving* direction. As he released the young girl from the handcuffs and freed her to live, he was grateful that he had gotten such a timely word.

Dom knew that he had also been freed from the anguish and torment that would have accompanied trigger pull. Would he have continued being a police officer if he had pulled the trigger? He didn't think so.

Dom had been ready for anything that shift, but couldn't have anticipated how grateful he would be for the spirituality that would save them both.

~

Many of us believe in intuition. Some may call it a sixth sense. Maybe some call it premonition. In the policing and military world, intuition might be called *Spidey-Sense* or other similar words to describe something that is above rational thought.

According to the Spiritual Research Foundation, sixth sense, or subtle perception ability, is our ability to perceive the subtle-dimension or the unseen world of angels, ghosts, Heaven (Swarga*), etc. "It also includes our ability to understand the subtle cause and effect relationships behind many events, which are beyond the understanding of the intellect. Extrasensory perception (ESP), clairvoyance, premonition, and intuition are synonymous with sixth sense or subtle perception ability"…This experience of the subtle-world is also known as a spiritual experience. [1]

Jeffrey G. Willetts, PhD, in his paper, "A Brief Introduction to the Language of Spirit and Law Enforcement" wrote, "*Evidentialism* is the idea that to be rational all true beliefs are subject to adjudication according to the strength of the evidence for or against. God's reality is not a physical reality. God is a spiritual reality. And it's only physical realities that are within evidentialism's purview." [2]

In the meta-physical, or mystical reality of spirituality, evidentialism gets left behind because it can't adequately explain the reality of mysticism. Mystery doesn't sound rational to those who haven't experienced it.

Police officers who tap into this sixth sense, intuition, or instinct can utilize it to save lives; crack a case; understand and respond to tactical situations properly; know what to say and when to say it; meet the needs of those they serve with compassion and humility; and be the catalyst for change. In short, they *tap into* a power that is exponentially released within them as they embrace the opportunities to serve that it provides.

---

* A higher plane in Hinduism

For Gandhi, "The best way to find yourself is to lose yourself in the service of others."

Some believe in guardian angels that are sent to help guide, protect, and speak to you. The mystic, Theresa of Avila, author of *The Interior Castle* and *The Way of Perfection*, called this inner voice, "Inner Locution."

For Theresa it was the voice of the Holy Spirit speaking internally in a way that stops all other thoughts, and compels the mind to listen.

For this mystic the reality of what was spoken interiorly was identifiable as God, and not a mental construct, if what was said helped comfort the soul, gave guidance, or was a prophecy that came to pass.

Fred Travis, PhD, defines spiritual experiences as those of wholeness—those of our universal nature, or that part of us not tied to time, space, or our individual bodies or personalities. Moreover, they are not confined to religious practices. [3]

For the Dalai Lama causality, or karma, is the law that governs the world of phenomena. A dynamic flux of changing appearances occurs, responding to causes and effects. [4]

Sun Tzu, in *The Art of War*, taught that the resources of those skilled in the use of extraordinary forces are as infinite as the heavens and earth; as inexhaustible as the flow of the great river. [5]

The key to take away is that we should, like Buddha, seek knowledge and wisdom our whole lives, so that our worldviews are informed with well-earned spiritual intelligence. As we allow our inner armor of spirituality to speak intuitively within, we will *tap into* a resource that creates a dynamic force for good. Those officers who avail themselves of this hidden spiritual fuel will be game-changers in the society they have been chosen and called to serve.

ENDNOTES:

1. Spiritual Research Foundation, "Sixth Sense."

2. Jeffrey G. Willetts, PhD, "A Brief Introduction to the Language of Spirit and Law Enforcement." (Quantico, VA: *FBI Law Enforcement Bulletin,* May 2009, Volume 78, Number 5), p.11.

3. Fred Travis, PhD, "Brain Functioning as the Ground for Spiritual Experiences and Ethical Behaviors." (Quantico, VA: *FBI Law Enforcement Bulletin*, May 2009, Volume 78, Number 5), p. 28.

4. Dalai Lama, *My Spiritual Journey* collected by Sofia Stril-Rever (New York, NY., Paris, France: HarperOne and Presses de la Renaissance, 2009, 2010), p.93.

5. Samuel B. Griffith, *Sun Tzu, The Art of War* (London, Oxford, New York: Oxford University Press, 1963), p.91.

CHAPTER 4

Virtue Alone Ennobles—Sola Nobilitat

*~Just as treasures are uncovered from the earth, so virtue
appears from good deeds, and wisdom appears from a pure and
peaceful mind. To walk safely through the maze of human life,
one needs the light of wisdom and the guidance of virtue.*

Buddha~

The chief was perplexed. An official complaint of inappropriate conduct by one of his senior officers alleged that the officer had pursued a married female clerk in the department he managed. The clerk's husband, who was a police officer, wanted the senior officer held accountable. To exacerbate the situation, the clerk and her husband had been going through an extremely difficult time dealing with a very sick child.

The husband who was complaining about the officer's conduct felt the senior officer had taken advantage of his vulnerable wife while he was her supervisor and was therefore aware of her family issues. To make matters worse, the clerk and the senior officer had been having sex at work, and there was little remorse for the actions by either the wife or the officer.

The actions by the senior officer and the female employee had led to a marriage separation in the complainant's family, as well as a breakup in the senior officer's family.

The chief knew that failure to take action of some sort would lead to his employees questioning his leadership qualities and would negatively affect employee morale. He knew that moving the senior officer to a new position would be a smart move as would be having a heart-to-heart with him about inappropriate conduct. He should also have this situation investigated thoroughly to get all the facts and then decide on appropriate action. It could involve demotion, negative employee citation, and even dismissal for cause.

But the chief knew that the real problem was his own behavior. He had left his own wife of thirty-five years and their three kids and had hooked up common-law with a young female officer. He had always had a roving eye, and it had gotten him in trouble more than once with his long-suffering and religious wife. She'd finally had enough and told him to get out of the family home. He was trying to keep his philandering quiet within the organization, and from the press, with pretty good success so far. Now this! What to do?

Those in upper and middle management knew of his wandering eye, especially the officer that was being complained about. These men had joined the job together over thirty years previously and raised many a pint, as well as chased many a skirt together. Good luck trying to lecture this senior officer about inappropriate conduct. The chief really didn't need to investigate the issue, when he knew the officer and his history as well as he knew his own.

How had he come to this point? He had all the professional accolades he ever wanted or had strived for, but had been rightly shunned by his wife and children as a fraud. The chief knew he couldn't even live up to one of the department's core values that he had helped draw up.

Of course he couldn't return to the religion of his youth, even though his conscience attacked him whenever he reflected on his life. To admit he needed to change how he lived life was one thing, and it was another to actually change his vices into virtues. He would have to deal with the hard reality of who he had become and be humbled. He had never been good with humble.

What choice did he really have? It was consensual sex after all. He was a busy man. He didn't have time for these types of frivolous complaints.

~

Most of us would agree with George Washington's statement, "I hope I shall possess firmness and virtue enough to maintain what I consider the most envious of all titles, the character of an honest man." The chief in this story failed to meet the test that Washington proposed. The reality is that all of us are on a journey of life that will test us continually on our willingness to pursue, with perseverance, the virtues that lead to being considered an honest person.

Many police departments have a list of virtues they call core values, and they expect the members of the organization to live up to those values. Unfortunately, there have been some in both management and the rank and file who have not lived up to those standards.

The result of officers not living up to core values is a department that is marred, embarrassed, and in turmoil within the organization and with regard to trust within the community.

Virtue is a general term that translates the Greek word *arête*. Sometimes *arête* is also translated as *excellence*. The moral theory of Aristotle, like that of Plato, focuses on virtue and the recommendation of a virtuous life leading to happiness. Vices are either a deficiency or an excess of human action or feeling. For Aristotle, the *Golden Mean* was the virtue between the vice of excess and the vice of deficiency.[1]

Eudaimonia is the state variously translated from Greek as *well-being, happiness, blessing* and in the context of virtue ethics, *human flourishing.* For the virtue theorist, *eudaimonia* describes that state achieved by the person who lives the proper human life, an outcome that can be reached by practicing the virtues.[2]

There are literally hundreds of virtues and vices in the moral, social, physical, and corporate spheres. Morals and virtues are nearly synonymous. They are the sentiments and values behind our ethical actions and rule-sets (they are the principles behind our code of conduct). Ethical behavior is action-based on the moral principles we call virtues.[3]

In considering virtues and their impact on our lives, it would be important to gauge the potential effects of vices, as well. Our ability to make choices for good or evil does not occur in a vacuum, since thoughts become actions, and actions affect us, as well as others within our sphere of influence. Marcus Aurelius' perspective was, "Such as are your habitual thoughts, such also will be the character of your mind, for the soul is dyed by the thoughts."

William J. Bennett, author of *The Moral Compass*, says ten traits of character could be identified:

1. Self-discipline
2. Compassion
3. Responsibility
4. Friendship
5. Work
6. Courage
7. Perseverance

8. Honesty

9. Loyalty

10. Faith

Bennett's basic assumption underlying life was that life was a moral and spiritual journey, and that we undertake it, at least in large part, to find our way morally and spiritually. [4]

He argues that wisdom and prudence are the virtues that power all the others, and that philosophers, theologians, and poets have long regarded wisdom as the sibling virtue of morality. If an individual is to do good, the tenets of the heart must be informed and directed by a well-ordered mind. In fact, the classical Greek thinkers regarded prudence as one of the fundamental virtues; to them, the word did not mean circumspection, as it does to us today, but rather the ability to govern and discipline oneself by use of reason. [5]

Through reason we can recognize the right choice in specific circumstances, and it is the intellectual virtue that makes it possible to put the moral virtues into practice. [6]

In practical terms, how then shall we live? What virtues do we find valuable for ourselves and believe to be true for all people? Why is a strong set of values rooted in virtues important when we face temptations and situations that are complex or seemingly obscure?

What vices do we find repugnant in others, and maybe more importantly within ourselves? Are we planning to do anything about our vices, or as leaders are we just going to concentrate on eradicating vices from those under our command?

What virtues, values, morals, and ethics are we willing to stand and die for? What do we have to do to ensure those self-same virtues become rock-solid values when we are under stress to vacillate? Are we willing to continue learning wisdom from various sources, secular and sacred, or do we know it all?

The philosophical and rabbinic methodologies of inquiry use questions to frame the issue. In our own case, it would be helpful to look at our vices, and then ask the question about whether we are comfortable with what is troubling our conscience. Do we have an informed conscience that can guide us? Should we heal ourselves before giving leadership and direction to others?

If a particular vice is something we want to change, then the next question asked should be; what is the corresponding virtue supposed to look like? How do we get to where the virtue becomes a habit?

As in any worthwhile endeavor, self-reflection and analysis can be painful. Thoughts become words, and words lead to action. We need to fundamentally change our vice-thoughts into virtue-thoughts actively and with perseverance (itself a virtue) to move our vices into hard-fought virtues.

What do we do with failure in this endeavor? We should be able to live with our past failures but be willing to try to do the right thing in the future. Cowardice in the interior person is the panacea of the weak. As the Dalai Lama says, "We can never obtain peace in the outer world until we make peace with ourselves." Confucius taught, "Our greatest glory is not in never falling, but in rising every time we fall."

Many people struggle with various vices that tempt them down the path of ruin in body, mind, and spirit. A false pride can seduce us with thoughts and words like:

- I deserve this.
- It's all about me.
- You don't meet my needs or expectations.
- What have you done for me today?

- Why should I extend myself for you?
- I deserved the raise and promotion and just did what I had to.
- It's not personal.
- They're so ungrateful and selfish.
- What part of "No" did you not understand?

Mahatma Gandhi taught that we should, "Always aim at complete harmony of thought and word and deed. Always aim at purifying your thoughts and everything will be well."

Jesus encouraged us to take the log out of our own eye before we remove the splinter from our brother's eye. In other words, self-reflection will allow us the opportunity to identify our own vices, while re-orienting our thoughts will lead towards the virtues we seek and desire.

Gandhi felt, "The best way to find yourself is to lose yourself in the service of others."

For Martin Luther King Jr., "To go forward, we must go back and rediscover those precious values – that all reality hinges on moral foundations and that all reality has spiritual control."

A review of history reveals a number of virtues that have been promulgated as important in the development of the human person and society:

- Honesty
- Truthfulness
- Compassion
- Tolerance
- Kindness
- Fidelity
- Selflessness
- Justice

- Prudence
- Temperance
- Courage

These are all virtues that have been identified throughout the ages as worthy of emulating.

Vices recognized are such as the following:

- False pride
- Avarice
- Greed
- Gluttony
- Hatred
- Calumny

Disordered passion has also been identified as having led to estranged relationships, crime, jealousy, terror, and war. The reality is that within our inner persons there is a war between the good intentions of virtues and the vices that entice us with their siren calls.

In the midst of this interior war are the influences for good that generally include our parents, teachers and education, religious affiliations, and spiritual practices.

The influences for evil may include bad friends, alcohol and other intoxicants, passions, desires, and the electronic devices that entice us into disordered behavior.

Internal peace is exhibited in external actions. Disordered desires lead to external actions that disrupt, maim, and destroy.

To have harmony in our souls we need to refuel our spiritual fuel tank *daily* so that our virtue doesn't break down at the side of the road of life. Then, when storms of life batter us and people look to us for leadership, they will easily determine whether we are worthy of their trust.

Actions speak of our convictions, our convictions speak of our virtues, and our virtues are on display through the values our actions display.

For the Greek soldier Xenophon, "The true test of a leader is whether his followers will adhere to his cause from their own volition, enduring the most arduous hardships without being forced to do so, and remaining steadfast in the moments of greatest peril."

Our soul requires constant spiritual tune-ups so that we can embrace a willingness to be a conduit for good. Spiritual practices can include meditation, reflection, prayer, rosary and prayer beads, reading sacred texts, learning from spiritual masters, attending a mosque, church, synagogue, temple, or silent retreats, communing in nature and engaging in other practices that enable our inner persons to be refreshed and renewed in harmony, balance, and peace.

Knowledge stimulates virtue, and virtue reflects knowledge. [7]

"Instruct a wise man, and he becomes still wiser; teach a just man, and he advances in learning."

(Proverbs 9:7 NAB)

The inner person requires spiritual wisdom to learn, grow, and inform the outer person. Spirituality is our inner body armor. As we grow in wisdom and interior strength, we can transform our thoughts and actions into the virtues that infuse our worldview and life journey.

As Mahatma Gandhi said, "You must be the change you wish to see in the world."

ENDNOTES:

1. Parry, Richard, "Ancient Ethical Theory." *The Stanford Encyclopedia of Philosophy* (Fall 2014 Edition), Edward N. Zalta (ed.)

2. Goodman, Lion, "The Master List of Virtues." belief closet.com

3. DeMichela, Thomas, "Vices and Virtues Explained" Sept 2, 2016, factmyth.com

4. Bennett, William J. *The Moral Compass,* (New York, London, Toronto, Sydney, Tokyo, Singapore: Simon &Schuster, 1995), p.4.

5. Ibid, p.13.

6. Ibid, p.13.

7. Procopius of Gaza, Bishop, "Commentary on the Book of Proverbs." Cap.9: PG 87-1, 1299-1303 *The Liturgy of The Hours,* Weeks 1-17 (New York: Catholic Book Publishing Co., 1975), p.211.

CHAPTER 5

Leadership by Example—Ductus Exemplo

~I cannot trust a man to control others who cannot control himself.

Robert E. Lee~

Sergeant Doug Harper was looking at Inspector John Hannahan walking calmly through the fire of the gas bomb that had been lit for training purposes for the 120 crowd-control officers. Hannahan, in his Nomex fireproof coveralls, gloves, boots, and helmet, was proving by example that the safety equipment they used would work. His boots were melting a bit but the inspector liked to lead from the front lines.

With G-8 coming to the city, the crowd-control officers had been getting plenty of additional training in crowd management strategies. Doug had twenty officers under his command, and in the chaotic conditions of riots they operated more like a military unit than a police detachment. Doug needed to know that his troop would stand fast when needed and would move as an integrated unit when he gave a command. He had to constantly assess the officers for stress-related cracks in their demeanor or behavior. An officer who lost his or her discipline on the front line could cause the line to cave in under pressure from the heaving crowd. You were only as good as your weakest member, and so there had been a lot of training involving the "crowd" trying to provoke the officers into losing their cool. For training purposes, the crowd was made up of civilian volunteers and in some cases military personnel.

The military personnel really enjoyed baiting the cops and loved to throw themselves at the police lines. Broken bones and other injuries didn't seem to slow them down much, although the deployment of tear gas and pepper spray didn't seem to be as enjoyable to them.

Doug felt confident with the overall leadership of Inspector Hannahan. He was a man who could be trusted. Here was an authentic leader who derived respect from his men, not because of his place in the command structure, but because he cared for his men and women and met their legitimate needs. The men and women of the crowd-control troops would walk through fire and hell for a man like the inspector.

Doug wanted to lead his troop with the same concern and sacrifice of service for his officers. He knew he would have to be a positive influence and earn the right to lead when he extended himself for the team and led with fairness, courage, and intelligence under fire.

G-8 arrived to the fanfare of the media from around the world. Multiple jurisdictions sent their crowd-control teams to the city to assist in crowd management and to keep the peace. They did some cross-training to ensure everyone was on the same page and looked forward to using their training in a real-life scenario.

They were deployed to a staging area where the command center had indicated a protest crowd was going to be, and they waited. In the ninety-degree heat the black gear they were wearing was threatening problems with heat stroke. A nearby empty building had a caretaker who agreed to put on the air-conditioning for them. Doug had another member get water and food for the troop and had them remove some of their gear to cool down. Washrooms were found and used by the troop prior to deployment. Doug knew he would get at least five minutes of warning from the command center if a crowd formed. The troop appreciated the gesture, and Doug was confident that, when the summons came to deploy, they would be fed and watered and ready to go.

The summons came for deployment and the troop lined up and marched to the area indicated to prevent crowd access into the building. They used the bike unit to keep pace with the crowd and when the crowd tried to force its way into various buildings, the unit interlocked the bikes as a mobile barrier. If the crowd got through the bikes, the crowd-control team would repel them.

The line held and the discipline by the crowd-control troop ensured that there were no breakdowns in the shield wall. When Officer Joey Waters started exhibiting agitation at the protesters yelling at him, Doug pulled him from the line for a cool-down and inserted one of his snatch-team members into the breach.

Leadership meant that you made decisions that were best for the team and although Joey didn't like being taken out of the line, he understood who the boss was. After a chat and a fifteen-minute rest with a water break, Joey was ready to be reinserted into the line. The chat had involved talking about putting on his game face and not reacting to the crowd. Professionalism under fire was a true test for everyone on the team.

G-8 ended with no injuries to their team. Doug was grateful that the troop did so well. Preparedness and training, along with a strong willingness to keep the peace, had brought success. The troop had trusted him with leadership, and he felt honored to have had their trust. Together they had respected the citizens' right to lawful expression and assembly while enforcing laws that kept lawbreakers at bay.

~Character-building begins in our infancy and continues until death.

Eleanor Roosevelt~

Chief Robert Moore leaned back in his ergonomic leather chair and pondered what to do. His homicide detectives had just told him that it was a clean, justifiable shooting.

Officer Phil White had been driving downtown to HQ from an outlying district office when he was flagged over by citizens, who told him there was a deranged Hispanic guy stabbing people on the sidewalk. Phil noticed blood-splatter on the sidewalk leading into an office building. When he looked into the front lobby area, he saw a group of people in a room just off the lobby clustered around a white male who appeared to have been stabbed in the abdomen.

Several people pointed towards the back of the lobby and said the guy with the knife had just gone in that direction. When Phil looked farther into the lobby, he saw a male rushing towards him with a knife in his hand. When Phil yelled at him to stop the male stabbed him twice in the chest area with his knife. As Phil fell backward, he drew his service revolver and shot the assailant twice in the chest.

The people assisting the stabbed pedestrian rushed to assist the badly wounded police officer. The man with the knife was dead. The group happened to have been taking first-aid training in the room off the lobby, and now they had two victims with serious stab wounds to the chest. Additional officers and paramedics rushed to the scene and the surviving men were transported to the emergency room at the Holy Cross Hospital, which had trauma teams standing by.

The chief was in a quandary. His deputy chiefs weren't all that helpful in giving advice. The dilemma was that police had recently shot and killed several males in a drug-induced gunfight in a major eastern city and the national press was using the race card as the reason for the shooting. Now his city had a shooting of a Hispanic male by a white police officer, and the chief was concerned about the reputation of the police department and of his leadership.

Sure enough, at the press conference the next day, reporters asked the chief if the shooting was racially motivated. He assured the press that the matter was being fully investigated and the results would be available when the police department had concluded the investigation. At that time, they would make a decision on whether it was a justifiable shooting or whether the officer would be charged criminally.

As he watched the news conference of the chief on TV, Officer Phil White lay on his hospital bed swathed in bandages and thought to himself, *What a wimp.*

Recently the chief had been interviewed about the most significant event he had experienced when he'd worked the street. He had replied that when he'd walked the beat as a rookie, it had been upsetting when a drunk had urinated on his uniform pants.

This was the leader that was going to make decisions about White's future?

It was bad enough that White had been forced to defend himself after getting stabbed twice, but then when he'd come to consciousness he'd found he had no support from the police department. Luckily, he had survived and could still take care of his wife and little boy. But the chief had decided to not visit him in the hospital because he had been concerned it might taint the investigation.

What leadership?

~Odious to the Lord and to men is arrogance.

Sirach 10:7 NAB~

Today the command and control paradigm of leadership is on the way out. For many that style had its place in history, but like the dinosaur its time is over, and for many it's good riddance.

Leadership in our modern world requires persons of good character, integrity, and virtue. While it is true that you can fool some of the people some of the time, you can't fool all the people all the time. Leaders who may initially appear to be people of character show their true colors when stress and difficult decisions need to be made.

Abraham Lincoln said, "You cannot escape the responsibility of tomorrow by evading it today."

Martin Luther King Jr. said, "A genuine leader is not a searcher for consensus but a molder of consensus."

Today's leader must have a sense of vision and the ability to cast that vision in a way that motivates, inspires, and creates change for the better. If the leader has vision and the charisma necessary to promote the vision but lacks character, the vision is doomed to failure.

James Hunter in his book, *The Servant* defines *power* as the ability to force or coerce someone to do your will because of your position or your might, even if they would choose not to. He goes on to define *authority* as the skill of getting people to willingly do your will because of your personal influence. [1]

Hunter says that power can be given or taken away, but authority is about who you are as a person, your character, and the influence you've built with people. [2]

Leadership is defined as a skill of influencing people to work enthusiastically towards goals identified as being for the common good. [3]

Leadership begins with the will, which is our unique ability as human beings to align our intentions with our actions and choose our behavior. With the proper will, we can choose to love, the verb, which is about identifying and meeting the legitimate needs, not wants, of those we lead. When we meet the needs of others, we will, by definition, be called upon to serve and even sacrifice. When we serve and sacrifice for others, we build authority or influence, called the *Law of the Harvest*. When we build authority with people, then we have earned the right to be called leaders. [4]

In his book, *The Speed of Trust* Stephen Covey tells us that trust is a function of two things: character and competence. *Character* includes your integrity, your motive, and your intent with people. *Competence* includes your capabilities, your skills, your results, and your track record. Both are vital. [5]

Len Marrella says in his book, *In Search of Ethics,* that character is manifest in decision-making and action. Ethics that guide action and decision-making are essential for trust – that's why we need leaders of character. [6]

General Matthew B. Ridgeway taught that character is the bedrock on which the whole edifice of leadership rests. It is the prime element for which every profession, every corporation, every industry searches in evaluating a member of its organization. With it, the full worth of an individual can be developed. Without it – particularly in the military profession – failure in peace, disaster in war, or at best, mediocrity in both will result. [7]

In his book, *The West Point Way of Leadership,* Colonel Larry R. Donnithorne (Ret.) said, "Character is a prerequisite for greatness. Leaders of character create organizations of character." [8]

Ralph Waldo Emerson is quoted as saying, "The force of character is cumulative."

Thomas Jefferson offered, "God grant that men of principle be our principal men."

Heraclitus summed it up with, "A man's character is his fate." [9]

Trust and truth are the cornerstones of character and go a long way toward building a bridge of character, which helps us transcend from success to significance. [10]

What happens when trust is abused? The following true story (name changed) may shed some light on that question:

Police officer James Rogers had moved from England to Canada to work in a major police department. After twenty years on the force in England and four years in the Canadian city, Rogers felt he was finally settling in. When the call came that his father had died in England he was devastated. He had felt a bit guilty coming to Canada, but his father had urged him to go and pursue his dreams. Rogers had two sisters in England who helped his father, but as the only son and eldest sibling he felt the responsibility to help as well. He needed to get home to help his sisters plan the funeral and set his father's affairs in order.

When Rogers approached his team sergeant with a compassionate leave request, the sergeant told him he wouldn't approve it unless he saw an obituary notice. Officer Rogers was crushed. He shouldn't have come to Canada. Why hadn't the sergeant shown some support and compassion? Why was the man so invested in process over empathy? Rogers wanted to quit.

~

The number one reason people leave their jobs is a bad relationship with their boss. [11]

The key to leadership is accomplishing the tasks at hand while building relationships. Trust is the glue that holds relationships together. [12]

Famous football coach Vince Lombardi said, "I don't have to necessarily like my players and associates, but as the leader I must love them. Love is loyalty, love is teamwork, and love respects the dignity of the individual. This is the strength of any organization." [13]

Love is how we ought to behave well towards others.

James Hunter stated, "I cannot always control how I feel about other people, but I certainly am in control of how I behave toward other people." [14]

General Douglas MacArthur prayed, "Build me a son, O Lord, who will be strong enough to know when he is weak and brave enough to face himself when he is afraid; one who will be proud and unbending in honest defeat and humble and gentle in victory."

Some of the character traits of a good leader include:

Patience – showing self-control in the face of adversity. [15] Leaders need patience because governing often consists in knowing how, with patience and affection, to draw good out of people. [16]

Discipline – to teach or train. [17] When we correct others in a manner that respects their personhood, we build trust into the relationship.

Kindness – giving attention, appreciation, and encouragement. Active listening requires a disciplined effort to silence all that internal conversation while attempting to listen to another human being. This identification with the speaker is referred to as empathy and requires a great deal of energy. [18]

Humility - being authentic and without pretense or arrogance. What we want from our leaders is authenticity, the ability to be real with people. [19]

A humble person is more concerned about; what is right than about being right; acting on good ideas than having the ideas; embracing new truth than defending outdated positions, building the team than exalting self; and recognizing contribution than being recognized for making it. [20]

Respectfulness – treating others as important people.
Leaders must make the choice about whether or not they are willing to extend themselves for those they lead. [21]

Selflessness – meeting the needs of others. [22]
Albert Schweitzer said, "I don't know what your destiny will be, but one thing I know: the only ones among you who will be happy are those who have sought and found how to serve." [23]

Forgiveness – giving up resentment when wronged.
We must practice assertive behavior with others, not passive doormat behavior or aggressive behavior that violates the rights of others. Assertive behavior is being open, honest, and direct with others but is always done in a respectful manner. [24]

Forgiveness allows one to reflect on the fact that we all fall short of the mark at times and understands that mercy triumphs over justice.

Honesty – being free from deception.
Honesty is about clarifying expectations for people, holding people accountable, and being willing to give the bad news as well as the good. [25]

From honest and ethical conduct comes trustworthiness; from trustworthiness comes respect; and when we respect each other we are fair and just. This is the key to peaceful and harmonious, productive human relations. [26]

Commitment – sticking to your choices.
True commitment is a vision about individual and group growth along with continuous improvements. When we choose to love, to extend ourselves for others, we will be required to be patient, kind, humble, respectful, selfless, forgiving, honest, and committed.

These behaviors will require us to serve and sacrifice for others. When we serve, and sacrifice we build authority with people. [27]

One of the fastest ways to restore trust is to make and keep commitments – even very small commitments – to ourselves, and others. [28]

Moral Authority.

The most powerful and enduring force for any leader is moral authority. One may have constitutional authority or positional authority and charisma, but these without moral authority are vacuous. Moral authority comes from trust and with trust there can be great synergy. Do not underestimate the power and value of moral authority. [29]

With moral authority a leader also has great responsibilities.

Most unfortunately, we seem to be embracing the misperception that tolerance of human differences in race, culture, ethnicity, religion, or political persuasion suggests that we should be tolerant of unethical practices, as well. [30]

What about core values and a mission statement for the organization?

The reality is that people buy into the leader before they buy into a mission statement. [31]

A leader progressing in integrity will use three *accelerators*; make and keep commitments to yourself, stand for something, and be open – these will help increase your integrity. [32]

For Stephen Covey, leaders need to be congruent. "When he or she is whole, seamless, the same-inside and out. I call this congruence." [33]

Another payoff for the leader would be a life of spiritual congruence. If we are truly leading with authority, extending ourselves for others, we will be following the Golden Rule. [34]

In matters of what is *good* there is a commonality among humans. We tend to believe in a *natural moral law*; and it has been discovered. The Greek philosophers (Socrates, Aristotle, Plato), the Talmud, the New Testament, the Koran, and the doctrinal guidance of essentially all religions and cultures teach the Golden Rule and extol justice, mercy, respect, and similar values. Unfortunately, we do not always practice what we believe to be ethical and moral. [35]

A leader is someone who identifies and meets the legitimate needs of their people and removes all the barriers, so they can serve the customer. Again, to lead you must serve. [36]

In the policing world, the customer is the public. Citizens extend trust to the police to serve them and to be an instrument of justice in society.

The *Public Trust* in the police as guardians of society has been eroding in the past decades and it is up to police leaders to work diligently to regain this trust.

Police must keep their commitment to public safety by cleaning up their own house. When police refuse to investigate crimes or treat citizens with apathy, disdain, arrogance, or brutality, it begets antagonism, and the charter and mandate to be peacekeepers and guardians of society is eroded.

What are the legitimate needs of the officers on the front lines that have not been addressed properly, and are creating unnecessary stress? What can be, and should be done, to serve officers of all ranks? The following areas of concern seem to have commonality throughout multiple jurisdictions: There seems to be a near-universal wish to:

1. streamline and reduce paperwork. In many jurisdictions' front line, officers are serving the *paperwork system,* which

is eating up significant on-duty time that could be spent investigating crime.

2. support officers facing internal disciplinary measures and to significantly quicken the procedure to reduce stress to the officer and family.

3. ensure unnecessary court procedures are reduced especially with officers on night shift, through on-going dialogue with the justice system.

4. train supervisors in active listening, empathy, and leadership-by-example skills to enhance job retention and reduce cynicism, and poor performance.

5. ensure family members are aware of the EAP (Employee Assistance Programs) available to them, and develop easy access to resources through innovative technology to reduce family stress.

6. develop promotion processes that are fair and impartial as well as implement a speedier process to make it cost-effective and reduce stress for those involved in seeking promotion.

7. promote *vocation* and *mission* to reinvest officers in their call to serve and protect the public with humility, respect, compassion, mercy, and willing service. It should be ensured that *all* crimes are diligently investigated to the fullest extent possible so that the *public trust* is regained. The "broken-window policy" in New York City is a good example of significant crime reduction that ensued when police investigated what in the past had been considered minor crimes that didn't need investigating.

8. ensure that commanders and leaders at the top are being guided and following the highest standards of ethics and morality to *earn* the right to lead the men and women who serve and protect. It should be ensured that a two-tiered

system of accountability is eliminated. Fairness and discipline should be consistent throughout the organization to regain trust internally. The chief must be a person of *moral authority* who is entrusted with the responsibility to lead by example, and who should insist the same from everyone in the organization.

9. that the calling to *serve* must take precedence over *being served* at all levels of the organization to engender a culture of trust within the organization and with the citizens that bestow the *Public Trust.*

10. promote the physical, mental, and spiritual wellness of all officers through facilities, training, and the use of both internal, and external resources, should be a priority.

In *Leaders,* Warren Bennis, and Burt Nanus indicate that leadership is not so much the exercise of power itself as the empowerment of others. [37]

The surest way to harness the collective genius of all the people in any organization is to create and communicate a vision based on shared values promoting trust and fairness. Integrity and honesty foster trust, and trust enables commitment, and commitment produces synergy, and synergy produces superior performance. [38]

People who are congruent act in harmony with their deepest values and beliefs. They walk the talk. [39]

Jack Trout said, "At the end of the day, people follow those who know where they're going."

Franklin Delano Roosevelt said, "It is a terrible thing to look over your shoulder when you are trying to lead and find nobody there." [40]

A police leader who has inner harmonic congruency will have the tranquility, balance, joy, happiness, and peace to lead with a servant's heart. Servant leadership is peacemaking. The spiritual fuel necessary for great sacrifice will come to those who seek wisdom. Mahatma Gandhi taught, "The law of sacrifice is uniform throughout the world. To be effective it demands the sacrifice of the bravest and most spotless."

Leaders who have cultivated the inner armor of spirituality will find that humility and courage will emanate in the outer person. Leaders of influence have wisdom, insight, vision, and a mission to serve in such a way that their authenticity is a reflection of their inner harmonic congruence. Their burning desire to serve will change the world.

ENDNOTES:

1. James C. Hunter, *The Servant: A Simple Story About The True Essence Of Leadership* (Roseville, CA: Prima Publishing, 1998), p.30.

2. Ibid, p.31.

3. Ibid, p.79.

4. Ibid, p.89.

5. Stephen M.R. Covey, *The Speed of Trust: The One Thing That Changes Everything* (New York, NY: Free Press, 2006), p.30.

6. Len Marrella, *In Search Of Ethics: Conversations with Men and Women of Character* (Sanford, Florida: DC Press, 2008), pp.285, 294.

7. Ibid, p.293.

8. Ibid, p.301.

9. Ibid, p.303.

10. Ibid, p.175.

11. Covey, *The Speed of Trust*, p.12.

12. Hunter, *The Servant*, pp.41, 45.

13. Ibid, p.91.

14. Ibid, pp.96, 98.

15. Ibid, p.101.

16. Francis Fernandez, *In Conversation with God*, quoting J. Escriva', *Furrow*, p.405 (London, New York, Nairobi, New Delhi: Scepter, vol. 3, 1994), p.330.

17. Hunter, *The Servant*, p.102.

18. Ibid, p.103.

19. Ibid, p.111.

20. Covey, *The Speed of Trust*, p.64.

21. Hunter, *The Servant*, pp.112, 114.

22. Ibid, p.116.

23. Marrella, *In Search of Ethics*, p.256.

24. Hunter, *The Servant*, p.117.

25. Ibid, pp.118, 119.

26. Marella, *In Search of Ethics*, p.198.

27. Hunter, *The Servant* pp.119-122.

28. Covey, *The Speed of Trust* p.13.

29. Marella, *In Search of Ethics*, p.296.

30. Ibid, p.270.

31. Hunter, *The Servant*, pp.174-175.

32. Covey, *The Speed of Trust*, p.72.

33. Ibid, p.62.

34. Hunter, *The Servant* p.176.

35. Marella, *In Search of Ethics*, p.283.

36. Hunter, *The Servant*, p.64.

37. Marella, *In Search of Ethics*, p.300.

38. Ibid, p.314.

39. Covey, *The Speed of Trust*, p.62.

40. Ibid, p.106.

CHAPTER 6

May I Not Shrink From
My Purpose—Incepto Ne Desistam

"A cadet will not lie, cheat, or steal or tolerate others who do."

West Point Honor Code~

Officer Gord McDonald's job was to serve and protect all ten thousand citizens of the town. How could he do that when he trusted only one other officer in the ten-man department? Gord was pretty sure Corporal Don Macleod felt the same about him.

Moving from big city policing to a small police department in the foothills with great skiing, lakes, fishing, and hot springs had seemed like a smart move at the time, but it didn't take long to figure there were serious issues in this town. It had its funny moments, though.

John Springer was down at the pool hall trashing the place. At six feet nine inches tall and three hundred pounds, he took up a lot of space. Gord looked at his five foot two-inch partner, Paul, and said, "This should be fun."

When they got there the manager looked relieved and said, "Big John didn't like it when I told him to stop drinking beer in here."

The officers could hear the crashing of furniture and they came up with a plan. Officer Paul Martin would come in low and Gord would come in high and try to tackle Big John. But when they put their plan into action, they both got grabbed and launched like a couple of pygmies in a pygmy-tossing contest.

Thankfully, Big John got tired of throwing them and told them he was ready for jail. When Gord politely asked if he could hand-cuff him, Big John put his wrists together and said, "Good luck."

Big John's wrists were huge. No way the officers were going to get the cuffs on him, so why bother? Getting him into the back of the police car proved to be another challenge. The silent patrol-man shield** didn't leave a lot of room in the back seat, but they managed to stuff him in. John spent the night in jail for being drunk and disorderly and was released in the morning.

A week later a call came in from the Esso station. The clerk had reported an armed robbery. When Gord asked him what had happened, the clerk said, "Big John came in with a paper bag on his head with the eye holes and mouth cut out and he had a butcher knife in his hand. He asked me for money and so I said, 'Ok John. How much do you want?' Big John said twenty bucks should do it as he wanted to buy a box of beer. When I gave him the twenty he said, 'Thanks,' and left."

Gord asked the clerk how he'd known it was Big John. "Well, we've had plenty of beers together at his trailer up at the Big Sky Trailer Park on the hill. Plus, he's like, the biggest guy in town!"

Not long after that, Gord confronted Big John at the trailer park and Gord asked, "Big John, why did you rob the Esso?"

"How did you know it was me?" he asked.

** A plexi-glass and steel partition between the front and rear seats

"Well you see, John, you happen to be the biggest guy in town and Terry at the Esso recognized your voice. Now where is the beer you bought?"

"Can I finish this beer before you take me in?"

"Sure, no problem. Where's the rest of the beer?"

"Can't I keep the beer?"

"No. I've got to take the evidence with me. Do you mind pointing out the knife to me?" When Gord asked Big John if he could put the cuffs on him, John just shrugged. Gord looked at the man's wrists and remembered the problem. After searching John, he stuffed him into the police car again and drove off to the station.

Things went downhill when Gord arrested the circuit judge's best friend and drug dealer.

Marcel Owen owned one of the two ambulance companies and one of the two security companies in town. His wife had worked at the police department as a secretary until recently. The department had strong suspicions that Owen monitored the police frequency on night shift and did surveillance to determine where the one-man night shift car was.

Owen would take his security van into the industrial area, use a slingshot with ball bearing ammo, and break the big windows on the commercial structures. He would then go around the next day and "suggest" that the owners consider installing his security system with a monthly monitoring fee to ensure the damage wouldn't continue. After all, a six by six-foot window cost over $1,000 dollars to replace. He would remind them that the town police couldn't be everywhere, and his monitoring occurred 24/7.

Most of the business owners saw this as a form of subtle extortion, but couldn't afford to keep replacing their windows. The police knew he was doing it however, they couldn't seem to catch him in the act. Most of the commercial break and enters could probably be laid at his feet, although as yet the police hadn't been able to prove it.

Informants told police that Owen was also involved in prostitution at the coal-mine camps outside town, as well as drug distribution. He was into armed robberies, and wasn't above using intimidation and violence to deter competition. When sending a message was needed, Owen used Gary, a large, heavy-set enforcer.

One night, Gord saw Owen's security van skulking around in the industrial area and decided to pull it over to determine what he was up to. When Gord walked up to the driver's door Owen refused to give his driver's license, and when Owen opened the driver's door yelling obscenities, a bottle of wine, partially empty, fell out. When Gord told Owen he was going to search his van for alcohol and drugs Owen refused to allow him to do so. Gord arrested him for obstruction of a peace officer in the execution of his duties, and then handcuffed and placed him in his police car.

Unfortunately, Gord didn't find any other alcohol, or B&E tools and the like, in the van. Owen was released on an appearance notice for court and that was when Gord had his first run-in with circuit judge, Tom Turner.

Judge Turner told Gord in no uncertain words that he had no authority to arrest Marcel Owen, and in fact the next time Gord arrested Owen he would go to jail.

Gord wondered how much time he would spend in jail if he backhanded the judge right off the bench. Sanity prevailed as Gord imagined his wife Julie and their two small children visiting him in jail.

Cpl. Don MacLeod took Gord aside to enlighten him. He told him that Judge Turner and Marcel Owen were best friends. Don confided that this could be because Owens supplied the judge and the two prosecutors in town with cocaine. The lawyer on retainer by the government to do federal prosecutions was also using coke. Don pointed out that most of the other lawyers in town were also into the cocaine.

Cpl. Don had compiled evidence on the judge and his lawyer friends as well as on members of town council who had been involved in questionable land re-zoning they had interests in. Don hadn't been too sure about a couple of police officers on the job either, and he didn't trust most of them.

It was hard for Gord to take in. It sounded like a movie on corrupt towns in the Southern States. How could this have happened? Didn't judges and lawyers take an oath to uphold the law and have a code of ethics to abide by? What about their oath of office when they swore to serve and protect, and enforce the law? What had turned these people away from their calling and vocation? Was it greed? Power? Was it because they could abuse their authority without any apparent consequences?

As a new officer in the department, Gord was crushed. What a mess! How was he going to do the right thing when the judicial system was corrupt, and Don wasn't even too sure of the reliability of several of the police officers?

Don wanted the two of them to stick together. They decided to notify the Solicitor General of their concerns of judicial impropriety, especially after a drug case Judge Turner had thrown out of court. An informant had let police know about two drug couriers coming into town on the Greyhound bus with two suitcases of marijuana and cocaine. Police had followed the couriers from the bus depot to the condo of husband-and-wife drug dealers. A search warrant was obtained from a justice of the peace and when the police went into the condo, the four suspects were weighing and bagging the marijuana and cocaine. All four were arrested and charged with possession for the purpose of trafficking in a narcotic.

The two out-of-town couriers pled guilty, received a sentence of two years less a day, and were transported to the closest institution, while the two local drug dealers pled not guilty.

Cheryl Moss, the federal drug prosecutor, got up in court and said, "Your honor, the prosecution offers no evidence."

Judge Turner replied, "Dismissed," and rapped his gavel on the pad.

Don looked at Gord wryly. Stupid out-of-towners should have pled not guilty. The local drug dealers supplied the federal drug prosecutor and the judge with cocaine, and it only took about ten seconds for the two of them to get rid of the case. The Solicitor General's office wasn't interested. They had appointed the judge, who had been a former prosecutor, as well as the current prosecutors. It would generate bad press.

Police credibility in town was at an all-time low. Even though they had a corrupt judiciary, the average citizen felt the corruption was the fault of the police. The government threatened to shut down the entire police department and bring it under federal control.

Gord and Don finally got a break. An informant let them know that when Marcel Owen and his nephew, Drew Owen, reported a B&E to a hardware store that Gord attended as the investigator, the Owens had actually taken the stolen rifles and shotguns to the paper mill and hidden them. They had then returned to the scene to report the incident. Later they had recovered the guns and went to Marcel Owen's house, where they had cut the shotgun barrels down to use in armed robberies.

As the investigator, Gord had taken down the names and serial numbers of the eight stolen guns and entered them on the national police database. No fingerprints of the culprits were found at the scene. He strongly suspected Owen and his nephew, but after the last go-around with the judge, didn't search the security van.

He and Don obtained a search warrant of Owen's house, and sure enough found all eight rifles and shotguns in the attached garage. Three of the shotguns had the barrels cut down, and the weapon-makes and serial numbers matched what had been stolen from Abe's Hardware Store.

Marcel Owen was arrested for break and enter and theft, as well as possession of restricted weapons. Marcel refused to talk to the police. The local press put the arrest on the front page of the weekly newspaper. The police and public heaved a sigh of relief.

An arrest warrant was issued for Drew Owen, and he was picked up by city police and shipped back to their town.

Gord told Drew Owen that he had the right to have a lawyer present for the interview, or any other person he wanted. Drew looked at him and said he didn't want a lawyer. He wanted to tell him what happened. Gord asked Drew if he could tape-record the interview and Drew agreed on tape to allow him to do so along with his refusal to have a lawyer present.

Drew had needed some money and his uncle, Marcel, had persuaded him to help out on the B&E at the hardware store. They had stolen the guns and hidden them at the mill because his uncle wasn't sure if the police would search his van. After reporting the B&E they had gone to the mill, recovered the guns, and taken them to his uncle's house. They had cut the barrels of the shotguns to do some robberies.

Drew had gotten scared and decided to take off and stay with some friends in the city. He had then been picked up and shipped back to his hometown.

The town police asked the Solicitor General, Thomas Gordon, for a prosecutor and judge from out of town, and Gordon agreed to their request.

The police needed a conviction to gain some credibility with their citizens. The case was a slam-dunk in terms of evidence. They were careful to put the court package together with the chain of custody, search warrant, testimony, and physical evidence.

All of the evidence was admitted. The search warrant was legal. The recovered stolen weapons were entered into evidence. The taped confession was admitted. But in his short summation, Judge David Peterman stated, "I cannot convict on the flimsy evidence of a co-accused. Not guilty." The fix was in.

Gord couldn't believe it. Another judge was refusing to do what his oath of office demanded. The Solicitor General had also sworn an oath of office. Why would they compromise the ethics demanded of them by the position they held in society?

Gord was sickened!

The government went ahead with their threat to shut down the police department. Inspector Bill Unger, the acting chief, was under orders from the town council to either persuade the police officers in the department to quit, or find a way to fire them for violations under the Police Act.

The police union wanted to fight the layoffs, and the town council just wanted the police to go away. They had a vested interest in getting rid of the police, because they feared their own land shenanigans would come to light.

Gord wanted to give up on policing this town, but he wasn't going without a fight. It was pretty hard to persevere when every day the acting chief was trying to charge him with a violation of the Police Act. Gord got to know the act really well, and after Unger tried to have him charged with disobeying a direct order, he finally told Unger in no uncertain terms to leave him alone. Unger had asked Gord by radio to fill out a traffic-accident report at the office. Gord was field training a rookie, Ron Anderson, and had him write up the accident report as part of his training while he caught up on some paperwork. When Unger later accused Gord of disobeying a direct order, he hadn't realized that the accident report had been done. It wasn't pretty. Gord didn't do well with bullies either on or off the job. Unger got the point.

Marcel Owen had let it be known through the grapevine that he was going to have Gord killed because the officer was following him around on night shift, and was putting a serious crimp in his operations.

Gord started carrying a weapon 24/7 and his wife Julie gave him the look. He explained the threat, and she was happy he had the sniper rifle, and handgun with him at all times.

Gord corralled Gary, Owen's enforcer, behind the high school to emphasize his own message. For some reason there was zero crime in town in the last month of town policing.

Gord could have stayed on with the federal agency in the town, but decided to go back to big-city policing. He figured that there would be more checks and balances. He hadn't seen any corruption the first three years of city policing, and the stress of policing in a corrupt town would be behind him.

The town made the big-city papers when an informant who had ratted-out Owen was found murdered on a forestry road north of town.

After a year back doing city policing, it felt good to be in the action, arrest the bad guys, and see them go to jail. In the city, over ninety percent of Gord's court cases ended in convictions, while in his town policing it had been only ten percent.

Judge Turner made the news as being voted the worst judge in the country by his fellow judges. Gord couldn't have agreed more with the assessment.

Gord's big-city squad wanted to go to the police bar when the shift ended. When they showed up they saw Cheshire-cat grins on the downtown, beat-cops' faces.

Gord needed to know what the story was. "Hey Jack, you look like the cat that got the canary. What's up?"

Jack Murphy, a tough and muscular beat cop, grinned and said, "Gord, wait till you hear this one. We see a government limo at that dive, the Imperial Hotel, so we go to the goof at the front counter and ask him about it. He says some older guy had a hooker on his arm, and was up in 207. So what we did was get ahold of Channel 7 News, and all the newspaper guys in the city. They set up on him just outside the doors of that sleazy hotel. When the guy comes out with the hooker on his arm, they hit him with the camera lights and mikes, and ask the *Solicitor General* what he's doing with the hooker. The guy replies that he is, 'Doing a one-man probe into prostitution!'

The patrol and beat cops all bent over in laughter, and Gord bought the beat guys a jug of beer. What a great way to end the day.

The next day the headlines blared, "Solicitor General Thomas Gordon doing a one-man probe into prostitution!"

Solicitor General Gordon was fired the next day. Karma?

Judge Turner was transferred to the city to do docket court. To show his displeasure, he tied up the process so badly that they had to keep moving him around. Turner called the city police one evening to report that his son Torrey had tried to stab him. He insisted his son be charged with attempted murder.

Torrey Turner, a convicted cocaine dealer, elected a jury trial. Judge Turner gave testimony, as did his son. The jury found Torrey not guilty.

~Make us to choose the harder right instead of the easier wrong and never be content with a half-truth when the whole can be won.

Excerpt from the West Point Cadet Prayer~

Those who have sworn an oath before God to serve and protect need to remind themselves constantly of their sacred calling as bearers of the *public trust*. Public trust and professionalism provide a bridge of respect between the police community and society, by which each may work with the other. Law enforcement is one vehicle whereby social order is maintained. If the police culture is unhealthy, then the result is detrimental to the wellbeing of our communities. [1]

Abraham Lincoln said, "If once you forfeit the confidence of your fellow-citizens, you can never regain their respect and esteem."

To choose the right we in public service need to constantly remind ourselves why we chose to serve our fellow citizens. Noble purpose requires noble thoughts. Noble thoughts lie in our inner world. If we don't reflect on service as a vocation, a special calling given to the guardians of society, we are prey to the worship of self.

The Dalai Lama teaches that the self, is the root of the mental poisons. [2]

Egocentric people simply do not know how to love. They are always out for what they can get because the only love they understand is self-love. Basically, the egoist despises everyone else. Pride is the real cause of egoism and selfishness. [3]

Selfless love is often misunderstood. It is not a question of neglecting oneself for another's benefit. In fact, when you benefit others you benefit yourself because of the principle of interdependence. [4]

How do officers maintain noble cause and purpose in a toxic environment?

In the, Leadership Secrets of Attila the Hun we read that a Hun's goals should always be worthy of his efforts. A Hun without a purpose will never know when he has achieved it. [5]

When fear knocks at the door of your mind, or when worry, anxiety, and doubt cross your mind, behold your vision, your goal. Think of the infinite power within your subconscious mind, which you can recall by your thinking and imagining, and this

will give you confidence, and power and courage. Keep on, persevere, until the day breaks and the shadows flee away. [6]

To maintain the right, we need to stay focused on our purpose
and not let supervisory pettiness, traumatic events, and the
reality of evil deter us from our sacred calling. Jesus said, "Blessed
are the peacemakers for they shall be called children of God"
(Matthew 5:9 NAB).

Always remember that worthy causes meet with the most resistance; even internal withholding of support and loyalty. If victory is
easily gained, you must reconsider the worthiness of your ambitions. [7]

When we make a commitment to stay true to our vocation,
mission, and purpose despite opposition from within our departments and from those we serve, we become part of something
bigger than ourselves. Every officer is a leader when bearing the
public trust as a sacred calling to serve and protect. Nobility of
character leads to noble actions that will build societies.

Those who shrink from this noble calling through fear and
frustration will be handcuffed in their desire to serve. Courage
is doing the right thing despite the fear. Society, to exist in peace
and security, needs people of courage to stand for the right.

ENDNOTES:

1. Jonathan Smith and Ginger Charles, "The relevance of spirituality in policing: a dual analysis" (*International Journal of Police Science & Management*, Volume 12, Number 3), p.333.

2. Dalai Lama, *My Spiritual Journey*, collected by Sofia Stril-Rever (New York, NY, Paris, France: HarperOne and Presses de la Renaissance, 2009-2010), p.100.

3. Francis Fernandez, "In Conversation with God, Daily Meditations." Volume 3, 50.2 (London, New York: Scepter, 1990), p.328.

4. Dalai Lama, *My Spiritual Journey*, p.107.

5. Wess Roberts, PhD, *Leadership Secrets of Attila the Hun* (New York, N.Y: Warner Books, 1990), p.106.

6. Joseph Murphy, PhD, *The Power of Your Subconscious Mind* (Toronto, New York, Sydney, Auckland: Bantam Books, 1963), p.199.

7. Wess Roberts, PhD, *Leadership Secrets of Attila the Hun*, p.89.

CHAPTER 7

Take Care of Your Own Self—Cura Te Ipsum

~Too long a sacrifice can make a stone of the heart.

William Butler Yeats~

Office Jerome Taylor felt like a vise was going to crush his head. The stress of trying to manage his professional and personal life was becoming more than he could handle. His father had pancreatic cancer and it didn't look good. To make matters worse, his father lived two hundred miles away and it was tough to get away enough because of shift work with the police.

His live-in girlfriend had left him because she said he was selfish and didn't meet her needs. She didn't explain herself too well and he wasn't sure what that meant.

The trauma and toxic evil at work had left him cynical and in despair. A recent call had really shaken him. Police had received a 911 call from a neighbor that something strange was going on at the Stavely house next door. The lights hadn't gone on in the house even though it was dark out and the neighbor's car was in the driveway.

When Jerome had gone to the middle-class home in the northwest suburb of the city, it was a horror show. Blood smeared the walls and floor, and he noticed a male in his early thirties lying in a pool of blood just adjacent to the main-floor bathroom. The male appeared to have a stab wound to the heart. A butcher knife was on the floor beside his right hand. Jerome felt for a pulse but didn't find one. He had seen these types of scenes before as a paramedic, but usually the cops had shown up first. Today he was the first one on scene.

Jerome called for backup as well as a sergeant and then noticed the shattered bathroom door half off its hinges. Blood was smeared on the walls and a woman in her thirties was lying sprawled on the floor beside the toilet. She had been stabbed numerous times in the chest. Jerome checked for a pulse, although he knew he wouldn't find one.

Jerome spotted a couple of kid's toys stacked against the wall leading into the kitchen and he felt sick. He didn't want to go upstairs, but what if a kid was injured? The stairwell walls going up the steps had also been smeared with blood. Because of the size of the palm print and the width of the smearing, it looked like a man's hand had done the smearing.

The blood trail led into a bedroom painted in pink. A blonde three-year old wearing her pajamas lay on the floor in a puddle of blood. She appeared to have been stabbed numerous times in the chest area and also didn't have a pulse. A rag doll was on the floor beside her in the puddle of her blood.

Jerome knew he had to keep searching, but every room was taking a chunk out of his heart. The next bedroom was painted blue and a six-year-old boy looked at him with sightless eyes. The boy had stab wounds to his arms and chest and had a look of shock on his face. Some of the slashes looked like defensive wounds. Another check for a pulse was negative.

Jerome knew he couldn't take much more.

The master bedroom looked like a disaster zone with clothing and pictures strewn on the floor. It appeared as if a major fight had happened there. No one was in the room, though, and Jerome quickly checked the bathroom and closets but didn't find anyone else.

He heard a yell from downstairs indicating his back up had arrived, recognized the voice of Officer Josh Turner, a one-year veteran, and told him to secure the outside perimeter. As one of the senior guys on the squad, Jerome didn't want to subject the junior guys arriving at the scene to the same trauma he was experiencing.

He still had to check the basement. It didn't look good when he saw the blood smears on the stairwell walls, and he dreaded what he would find. The basement had a suite with a small kitchenette, living room, and basement bedroom. The door to the bedroom was open and a young woman who appeared to be about eighteen was lying on the floor with her back against a narrow single bed.

Her throat had been slashed and her head was hanging by a thread. She also had multiple stab wounds to her chest and had bled out onto the floor. He checked the rest of the basement suite but found no more bodies.

The homicide detectives confirmed what Jerome had speculated. The father had wigged out and killed his wife, the kids, and the nanny in the basement suite. From all accounts the guy was a good family man, but for whatever reason he had lost it and killed his family and then himself.

How did you get to that crazy state? Jerome could see killing yourself, but killing your family didn't make sense. What kind of evil thoughts would lead to this action? The guy had no history of this kind of thing, and yet it had happened. Jerome knew he would have to live with this horror his whole life.

He wasn't feeling very good about himself either. He had tanked in his promotion interview and his career didn't look like it was going anywhere. His personal life was in shambles and there really didn't seem to be much to live for. Why bother, if the people you served didn't care? He felt pretty dark inside and he wondered if he could pull the trigger on his service weapon. One of the south-side guys had done it a couple of years earlier. Why not him?

As he left the district office, he started looking for a church. Maybe he would find some comfort if he could pray for a while. The Baptist church he drove by wasn't open on this Friday evening, and then he spotted a light on in the St. Joseph Catholic Church. A bunch of guys were going in and out of the church and he figured, *What the heck, let's take a look.*

Officer Scott Morrella was off-duty and helping to register men from across the region at the St. Joseph's Covenant Keepers men's conference that focused on being better husbands and fathers. He figured that he could use all the information and knowledge that was going to be presented over the next two days to enhance his own marriage. He prayed that these hundreds of men attending the conference would go home energized to be the best husbands and fathers they could be.

When Scott spotted Jerome, whom he knew from the precinct, standing in the middle of a crowd of men with that deer-in-the-headlights look, he knew right away that Jerome needed him. He turned over the registration desk to another volunteer, and then went to him and offered to go for a walk.

Jerome was a hurting unit and Scott listened attentively for over three hours as they walked for blocks in every direction. Scott knew that Jerome was a suicide risk. He registered his colleague for the weekend and decided he would keep him close for the entire conference.

Four other cops had also been organizing and volunteering at the conference and they all knew Jerome. They would all keep Jerome engaged in helping out at the conference and would lend a listening ear when he needed it. Jerome agreed to hang out with them and they all breathed a sigh of relief.

Scott asked Jerome if he could engage the police staff psychologist to talk to him, and Jerome agreed to see him the next week. Scott arranged for Jerome to stay at the Diakonos Retreat Society safe house for a while so he could be provided with meals and would have the space and time to regroup and rebalance his life. The attendant at the house was a retired nurse with a kind heart and listening ear. Scott knew she would be there for Jerome if he wanted to talk.

~To live happily is an inward power of the soul.

Marcus Aurelius~

The average age of death for a law-enforcement officer is ten to fifteen years earlier than the rest of the population. The divorce rate for police officers is twice that of non-law enforcement officers. The rate of substance abuse in the police culture is double that of the rest of society. [1]

According to the non-profit "Badge for Life" organization, research on suicides of police officers in America in 2017 was 140 persons; 96% were males and guns were usually used when the officers took their own lives. Their studies show more officers dying by their own hands than in the line of duty. The average age was forty-two with the average time on the job sixteen years. [2]

When you run these statistics past recruits in police training, you typically get a blank stare. In essence, it doesn't impact most of these young recruits, because they have little experiential knowledge of suicides or substance abuse although they may have experienced divorce in their families. As they put some years on the force, these statistics take on a more personal meaning.

Officers who experience critical-incident trauma that over-whelms their coping skills need a way, or method, to rebalance their lives. Critical Incident Stress Management (CISM) is one of the methods that have been developed to assist police, fire, EMS, medical staff, and the military to cope with trauma in healthy ways that can lead to rebalancing their physical, emotional, and spiritual wellbeing.

Mental health practitioners, peer support, debriefings, and defusings, as well as education, can all make a difference in helping persons recover from exposure to trauma. In essence, the better your coping skills, the more resilient you are to the negative effects of toxic trauma.

A strong family-support network, close friends and co-workers, pastors and leaders of faith communities, prayer, meditation, and an inner-armor spirituality that strengthens and renews balance, tranquility, and peace will all help in the wake of exposure to serious trauma.

Despite the many negative situations police officers encounter, the vast majority of officers are extremely resilient, demonstrating high levels of self-control, compassion, professionalism, and love for the work they have chosen. [3]

The problem remains, though, that some officers are falling through the cracks and feel that their only options are to leave their families, quit the department, drown their pain in substance abuse, or take their own lives.

There have been instances where an officer came home at the end of the shift to see his suitcase left by his spouse on the front lawn. Officers have been living in their vehicles, in barns, and in their partner's basements because they didn't want to end up in the single men's shelter.

Typically, marital conflict is accompanied by financial crisis. Many officers can't afford to stay at a motel or rent another place because finances are tight. If substance abuse is present, the specter of harming oneself looms.

Employee Assistance Programs (EAP) may or may not cover these additional expenses, but regardless, many officers choose not to use them for fear that the department managers may learn about their plight and promotion opportunities or transfers could be compromised. In essence, officers require utmost confidentiality about the things that affect them most personally and deeply.

For some officers, the straw that breaks the camel's back is a case for which they just have no coping skills or any capacity left. The well is dry, and things are not okay.

Who can I trust? Is there any hope left anywhere? Why did I think I could handle everything when this little thing has put me over the edge?

Why do so many spouses of officers feel that they get little support or education from the officers' departments in how to deal with non-responsive, non-communicative spouses? How do spouses deal with the effects toxic trauma have on their loved ones?

What type of support structure does the family have in dealing with shift work, court dates that interfere with family life, mandatory overtime, sleep deprivation, and officer fatigue that leaves no energy for families and results in communication and relational breakdowns?

Some departments sponsor spousal support groups, peer support groups, and chaplain programs to assist in meeting some of the needs of officer families.

Still, forces tend to emphasize the physical and mental wellbeing of officers but neglect their spiritual wellbeing. [4]

In their study "The Relevance of Spirituality in Policing," researchers Jonathan Smith and Ginger Charles indicate that the officers in the study spoke clearly about how their spirituality helps maintain their safety and creates space for unusual peace and growth in response to the evil experiences found in their work. The officers also reported that their spirituality provides opportunities to devote themselves to the communities they serve. [5]

Overall, little seems to be done by police departments on proactive education on the toxic effects of policing and strategies for healthy family life. When you factor in the training costs of transforming a civilian into a fully functioning and effective police officer, the value in preventing trauma-related attrition with education is clear.

Police officer and chaplain Kevin McInnes (Ret.) of the Calgary, Alberta Police Service, had a dream in which he saw a retreat center that could meet the needs of officers and their families for education, refreshment, and physical, emotional, and spiritual renewal.

He and his wife Deborah formed a team to bring this dream to reality and called the newly founded charity the *Diakonos Peace Officer Retreat Society*. *Diakonos* means *servant* and *minister* in Greek. Kevin felt that this was the role of the police.

Utilizing nearby retreat centers, halls, and schools and drawing on the expertise of local and international experts, the society conducted workshops on marriage enrichment, divorce recovery, step-parenting, family finances, retirement strategies, Critical Incident Stress Management for families, communication strategies, spirituality, compassion fatigue, secondary trauma, and emotional survival strategies.

In cooperation with the Calgary-based humanitarian NGO Mission Mexico and San Diego, California-based Amor Ministries, Diakonos was involved in taking teens and parents to the barrios of Tijuana, Mexico to build houses for the poor.

This allowed teens, their police-officer parents, and other emergency-service parents, to interact in positive dialogue while also doing a good deed for families in need. Those officers who had been separated from their teenagers due to a marital breakup also found this to be a time of renewal and healing of strained relationships.

A need for safe emergency housing for emergency-service personnel became apparent when stories of officers being kicked out of their family homes started surfacing. Many of these broken, wounded warriors had no place to go and often were at the end of their ropes emotionally, physically, spiritually, and financially. They were exhausted, crushed, and in despair. They needed a safe haven where they would have a roof over their heads, food to eat, and a compassionate, listening ear when they were ready. Police, EMS, and fire as well as military members needed this safe environment when their world seemed to be imploding.

Diakonos House was formed by the society with the help of the Calgary Police Association, who provided a building. A safe house was available for those who needed it. If finances were tight, even the very modest daily rate was waived. An attendant was hired to run the house, provide meals, and most importantly, offer a listening, compassionate ear.

Although many of the residents of the home were able to reconcile with their spouses, not everyone was able to do so. However, they all were able to take the time necessary to reflect, meditate, and avail themselves of the departmental and community resources necessary to restore some balance and harmony in their lives.

The safe houses extended to Red Deer and Edmonton, Alberta, over the next couple of years, as the need in those communities was identified. RCMP and outlying police services utilized the safe houses when there was a need for accommodating those in crisis as well as family members utilizing medical facilities in the cities.

The society's dream of its own retreat center has not yet been realized because of the significant costs associated with a purchase. There have been challenges in raising funds for this charitable organization, and most of the funding has come from corporate sponsors. Recently there has been a name change to the organization and they are now called *Legacy Place Society*.

What have been the results of this organization?

Hundreds of police officers, EMS, fire and military personnel, and family members have been assisted in learning how to cope with the toxic effects of stress in their professions through education, support, and safe housing.

Marriages and families have been restored, jobs have been saved, suicidal members have found meaning and purpose again, effective communication between spouses has brought the sparkle back into marriages, and lives have been changed for the better.

Can these initiatives be replicated worldwide?

The reality is that taking care of our own people is hard work, and often unappreciated. Persons that feel the "call" to serve those who serve are in the best frame of mind and spirit to create change. The challenge has always been to put the money, time, and effort where the passion in serving others is.

This initiative arose out of a spirituality infused with compassion. Needs that fell through the cracks required persons with a desire to serve those who were suffering.

Spirituality is the fuel that responds to unmet needs. Despite the challenges from some persons within and outside the department, this desire to help persevered.

Chief White Eagle, of the Ponca Nation, shared his wisdom over a century ago when he encouraged us with these words: "Go forward with courage. When you are in doubt, be still and wait. When doubts no longer exist for you, then go forward with courage. So long as mists envelope you, be still. Be still until the sunlight pours through and dispels the mists - as it surely will. Then act with courage."

In the policing world there is the saying, "We eat our own." Leaders without compassion or character create an environment of uncertainty and resentment in their sphere of influence. Taking care of people entrusted to you requires leaders with integrity, compassion, and the willingness to create a working environment that encourages the best efforts and genius of their people. When a leader's inner person is cured, the outer person can effect change. When a police department makes a commitment to properly care and encourage its own people, it can then take better care of the needs of the community it serves.

Serving the public is a noble calling. Nobility in a person is encouraged and strengthened with a clear understanding of vocation, mission, and purpose, as well as a willingness to engage the whole person, body, mind, and spirit in service to their families and the citizens of their communities.

ENDNOTES:

1. Jonathan Smith and Ginger Charles, "The relevance of spirituality in policing: a dual analysis." (*International Journal of Police Science & Management*, Volume 12, Number 3), p. 321.

2. "The Badge for Life" (published in Lawofficer.com)

3. Jonathan Smith and Ginger Charles, "The relevance of spirituality in policing: a dual analysis." p. 326.

4. Ibid, p. 320.

5. Ibid, p. 331.

CHAPTER 8

From the Heart—Ex Animo

~A coward is incapable of exhibiting love;
it is the prerogative of the brave.

Mahatma Gandhi~

W hat's the use? Annette left me for some New Age
cult to find herself and now the newspaper has laid
me off. I've become redundant in the new publishing world. You would think thirty years of loyal service in the
circulation department would count for something. They told
me it wasn't personal. They just couldn't afford my salary in the
downsized and reorganized master plan.

Losing the house because we couldn't afford the mortgage
payments didn't help. Annette blamed me for the whole thing,
and who could blame her? I had been drinking even more in the
last couple years to try to drown out the voices inside that kept
telling me I'm useless.

~

Officers Joe Adams and Cody Burns had worked as street partners
for the past six months and it had been a ride. Both men were the

same size; big men at 6'3" and 240 lbs., and they loved to be the first off at scenes to get into the scraps.

Cody looked sideways at his partner. Joe liked to ride in the passenger seat and had told Cody it was because he had to do so much driving outside the job. Joe liked being chauffeured around. They usually grabbed a van as it gave them more elbowroom. The smelly drunks didn't stink up the front as badly because of the wall between them and the prisoner cage.

Working with Joe was different than working with any of the other partners he'd had over the past ten years. Joe was a decade older and had been in a couple of police departments, and he didn't like the bullshit police politics any more than Cody did. He knew that Joe would be the first to kick a door down, and knew without a doubt Joe would back him up in a firefight to the death.

What Cody couldn't quite figure out was Joe's religion. For himself, he never gave much thought about any particular religion, although his mother had made him go to Sunday school as a child and had taught him the difference between right and wrong. He'd gone to live with his dad when his parents divorced. His dad didn't care much about religion, and Cody stopped going to church.

Until recently he had firmly believed that religion was a crutch for the weak and cowardly, especially in police work. In policing you didn't want a partner who was scared or refused to go into battle. Your life depended on the partner in the seat beside you, and typically you spent the first few shifts with a new partner getting a handle on how they thought.

Cody had been pretty surprised and pleased when he talked to Joe. Here was a cop who had gone through numerous battles successfully because he was mentally, physically, and spiritually tough. Joe was open about his spirituality, but didn't preach at Cody. He actually cared about the drunks, the poor, and the oppressed they encountered. Joe talked to the pukes they arrested, and got them to tell him their life stories. It was amazing how criminals who had been told by lawyers their whole lives not to talk to the cops, would open up to Joe and spill their guts.

Cody knew he himself was apt to be cynical by nature, and the job hadn't helped much. Working with Joe had made him think a lot about his own life. He tended to be selfish, according to the women he had bedded. Settling down with a wife and kids hadn't seemed that attractive until he had visited with Joe and his family. They seemed happy and it was obvious that there was lots of love in their house. He hadn't worked with any other partner who hadn't bitched about their wife and kids.

Just yesterday they had received a call from a traffic guy on Memorial Drive, who had stopped a motorist for speeding just outside the downtown core. Another driver had pulled up behind the stopped traffic unit and reported that some woman on the Fifth Avenue Bridge looked like she was going to jump into the river. The traffic guy put the call out on the radio, asking if anyone was close. Cody and Joe were only a half a block away and took the call.

They decided to park their police van at the bridge entrance so they didn't spook the woman who was leaning out over the center of the bridge span. Cody and Joe ran towards her, as she looked like she was going to jump any second. They got there just as she climbed onto the steel railing and launched herself off the bridge. They grabbed the woman in midair, pulled her back onto the deck, and handcuffed her.

That's what he meant! Timing was awfully cute here. A split-second later and they wouldn't have caught her. If the citizen hadn't talked to the traffic guy it would have been too late. If the traffic guy hadn't gotten on the air right away it would have been too late. If they hadn't been Johnnie-on-the-spot they would never have gotten there in time.

Coincidence? Working with Joe seemed to have a lot of them.

The jumper had a lot of problems. She had been sexually abused by her father and ran away at fifteen. She had gotten into prostitution and been a biker's momma. The heroin addiction had sucked the life out of her, and at thirty she looked about fifty. She had been stoned, and yet Joe had listened carefully to her all the way to the hospital and in the padded cell until she could see a psych doc. Cody figured she was a waste of skin and was anxious to hit the street. Joe was such a good guy, though, that he couldn't tell him that.

Cody wondered about himself. He usually had no problems telling partners what he thought. Joe was the total package – he cared about people and tried to help them. He could outfight anyone on the street, and was what was called a street monster. For street cops, that was the highest form of praise. Joe had the highest arrest rate of anyone downtown and cleared more files than all of the dicks downtown because he talked to the bad guys as well as the victims. His cred with the other cops was amazing. He would talk to a lot of guys and gals having supervisor problems, marital and relationship problems, and other issues.

Joe made Cody nervous. What gave him the street smarts? How come he was always the first guy at a call? Why did he have natural leadership qualities? Everyone looked to him for direction even when a sergeant showed up.

Last week was a perfect example. They had received a call from the Alleyway Nightclub. There was a naked guy eating the ceiling tiles. Cody and Joe were the third car-crew out so they weren't doing the paperwork, but went anyways. It's not every day you get to see some naked guy eating ceiling tiles, and the call sounded fun.

The other downtown cops and a couple of paramedics were standing in the basement men's room trying to figure out what to do. The naked guy was in a stall standing on a toilet seat eating the ceiling tiles and he looked stoned. He was a roid-monkey with muscles on his muscles. He was high on cocaine and, along with the steroids he had taken, was totally wacked out. Cody figured he would get a severe case of "ceilingitis" if he kept eating the tiles.

One officer suggested they pepper spray the guy, and the rest of them laughed. Go ahead and try to arrest the guy in that closed environment with nowhere for the pepper spray to go. Another cop suggested hitting him with a tranquilizer shot. The female paramedic just looked at him and said, "With what he's got in his system, it would probably blow up his heart."

Joe suggested that the three roid-monkey bouncers standing around should arrest their workout buddy and then hand him over to the cops. They shook their heads no. The bouncers wanted no part of it.

Everyone was at a bit of a loss. Joe and Cody looked expectantly at the first car-crew guys, waiting for them to take the lead in arresting this guy. The guys wouldn't meet their eyes. They knew that if this guy went stupid, cops like themselves could get hurt.

Everyone looked at Joe and Cody, and Joe turned to Cody and said, "You ready?"

Cody smiled and nodded his head. He figured Joe was going to use the doggie pile approach, but Joe went into the stall, grabbed the guy's left hand and put it into a reverse wristlock. He grabbed the other arm, put it behind the roid-monkey's back and slammed on the handcuffs. It had taken about three seconds and Cody hadn't even gotten into the bathroom stall. Talk about speed cuffing!

Everyone was extremely impressed. Joe handed off the guy to Cody, who tried to act nonchalant about it as he handed the goof to the sheepish car crew.

Joe was one of the senior officers there, but no one else had stepped up to the plate. Cody guessed that leadership meant leading by example, and Joe kept showing what it was supposed to look like.

Cody considered himself a pretty good cop. He didn't shy away from the rough stuff and could be counted on to do his fair share. Why did Joe always go beyond the call of duty? Why did he care so much? Was his concept of spirituality worth exploring? One thing was for sure – Joe was the most interesting partner he had ever worked with.

Joe had a unique sense of humor. Cody remembered the video camera Joe liked to take on night shift. Joe had interviewed him on video while they chased a stolen vehicle out of the downtown core. The pulsating emergency lights had bounced off passing buildings and the screaming siren had contrasted with the calm voice of Joe interviewing Cody about what his feelings were on the nature of the bad guy's thoughts, and actions. It was a hoot.

Joe's next brilliant idea with the video camera involved videoing a hooker in front of the Blue Lagoon Tavern and Hotel. The hooker was convinced that the world needed to hear her story. She seemed to somehow believe that they were part of the Los Angeles Police Tactical Video Unit helping out the local police.

The blue neon light of the seedy hotel made a great backlight as Cody filmed and Joe did the interview. As the woman related her sad tale of woe, an old lady showed up from the adjacent seniors' tower. She was there to help the street girls with cookies and related that she had just gotten a new, ninety-two-year-old boyfriend. She tittered behind her hand after Cody asked her if they were practicing safe sex.

Working with Joe was a constant surprise, and in the policing world they were closer than brothers.

Cody couldn't believe they were going to two suicide calls in two days. There was no way they could get to the heart of the downtown before all the other cars. They were out in the boonies and it would take at least six to seven minutes to get there. On a Friday night there were at least a half-dozen police cars in the downtown core.

Somehow they ended up being the first car at scene. A disc jockey from the radio station in the high rise beside a nine-story parkade had reported seeing a male on the top-floor-level cement railing, and it appeared he was going to jump.

The railing was at least a hundred feet above the railway tracks that bisected the downtown core.

Joe approached the male standing on the six-inch ledge, four feet above the parkade deck. He motioned Cody to stay back so they wouldn't spook the middle-aged man on the railing ledge. The man was swaying slightly with a bottle of whiskey in one hand and a large knife in the other.

"Hi sir. I'm Joe. Can I ask you what you're doing on the ledge?"

"What do you care?"

"I'm concerned, sir. Why don't you come off that ledge and we'll talk about it?"

"You don't care, you're the cops. You'll just arrest me and take me to jail."

"I'm Joe, and I'd like to know who you are. Will you tell me? Why are you up there? I'd like to know." Joe was trying desperately to establish some kind of rapport with this guy. A lot of times at suicide calls the person just wanted someone to listen to him or her. Most of them weren't overly serious about killing themselves. This guy looked like he wanted to jump.

"I'm Bert. I've got no reason to live. My wife left me for some New Age thing. My boss at the newspaper fired me, and my kids hate me. I'm done! As soon as that train comes, I'm jumping."

Joe looked to the west and sure enough he could see a train coming eastbound towards them. He noticed Bert put down his bottle on the ledge and somehow reach into his pocket for a cigarette and lighter without falling. Joe doubted he could do that on the narrow ledge sober, and yet, this half-drunk guy had somehow done it.

"Hey Bert, can I bum a smoke off you?" Joe knew that he had to keep Bert talking and the usual police stuff wasn't working too well

for him. Bert gave him a smoke, and Joe lit up. It was the first cigarette he'd had since his older brother had caught him in the wood
shed at fourteen and told him it was smoking or sports but not both.

Joe was running out of options and when Bert turned around
to look at the progress of the train, he decided to try to grab Bert
off the ledge. The keys on his duty belt jangled as he rushed
forward. He had forgotten to stuff them in his pocket.

"Get back!" Bert was brandishing the knife in his right hand.

Joe stepped back and put his hands in the air. This wasn't
going well. He knew he had to dig deep and speak to Bert from
the heart, and he threw a prayer heavenward.

"The train ain't coming!"

"Yes it is. I can see it coming."

"Bert, the train isn't coming because I asked God to stop it.
You see, God sent me here to talk to you. He loves you, and so do
I. Tell me what I have to do to get you off that ledge."

"Why do you care? You'll just arrest me and take me to jail."

"Bert. It's not a criminal offence to attempt suicide. What
happens is I will take you to the hospital and a doctor will see
you. You would probably be out in twenty-four hours. What's the
real reason you're on the ledge?"

"Officer, I just moved into subsidized housing on Seventh
Avenue and I can't pay the three hundred and fifty dollar rent.
What's the use of living? Everyone hates me, and even though I
paid my bills my whole life, I can't pay this. I'm useless, and if you
hadn't shown up I would have already jumped."

Joe knew he had to dig deep into his inner person and beliefs
to respond properly. Did he believe this man deserved to live with
hope? Did he have the compassion to find a solution for what was
happening right now? Was he willing to do the right thing here?
"Bert, I'm going to pay your first month's rent. I just happen to
have some spare cash because my brother repaid me for an airline

ticket I bought him ten years ago. What do you say? Come on down from the ledge. I promise you I will go directly to the bank ATM and get you the money. I'll take you to the hospital after that. What do you say?"

"Why would you do that for me? You're a cop. You guys don't make much money. You probably have your own family to feed. Why would you do that for me?"

"It's because I love you, Bert. God loves you, as well, and he sent me here tonight to tell you that. I'm a man of my word. Will you trust me?"

Bert looked at him for a long time with a quiet intensity that seemed to look into his soul. Would he see Joe as authentic, or just another authority figure? "Ok. I'm coming down."

Joe asked him to put the knife on the ledge, and then the two of them hugged each other on the parkade deck.

Cody shook his head in wonder. It had looked like the guy was going to jump a couple of times, but somehow Joe had talked the guy down. Cody had been too far away to hear their conversation clearly, but he had gotten hold of dispatch to get them to stop the train. If the train hadn't stopped, he was pretty sure the guy would have jumped.

He didn't know why Joe stopped at the ATM for cash, but they got the attempted jumper to the emergency room at the General. It made you think about things. Most guys don't save even one person trying to kill themselves in their entire careers, and here they had saved two people in two days. When he and Joe went for coffee he would have to ask Joe what he had told the guy.

~It is in our lives, and not our words, that our religion must be read.

Thomas Jefferson~

The Dalai Lama teaches that despite their different concepts and philosophies, all the chief religious traditions bring
us the same message of love, compassion, tolerance, temperance, and self-discipline. They also have in common their
potential to help us lead happier lives. [1]

Serving others from the heart means having a spirituality that
informs, animates, and fuels the desire for peacemaking.

In *The Peacekeepers,* retired police officer Michael Dye says that
God can use you in order to fulfill some special assignment that
will happen in a time and place only He knows. It may be to help
someone who needs physical life-saving. It may be to help bring
closure to a grieving crime victim. It may be to make an arrest
and remove someone from society. You could be the answer to
someone's prayers, and your actions may strengthen someone's
faith. On an almost daily basis you will be confronted by tragic
situations and circumstances. God can use you in these situations to make a spiritual difference by placing you at just the right
moment in someone else's life. [2]

For lawyer Ken Sande in *The Peacemaker,* if you believe that
God is sovereign and that he will never let anything into your life
unless it can be used for the good, you will see conflicts not as
accidents but as assignments. This kind of trust glorifies God and
inspires the faithfulness needed for effective peacemaking. [3]

Kevin McInnis, a retired police officer and chaplain in *The
Servant Warrior-The Role of Faith in Policing* explains that for a
peace officer whose feet are ready to move into the battle against
evil, a faith that depends on the perfect love of God can bring him
to a place where he lives out a sound, trained mind, a love for his
neighbor, and a disciplined lifestyle.

When he experiences fear – and he will – love drives it out
and he acts courageously to do the right thing for the sake of the
oppressed, the imprisoned and chained, the less fortunate, the

poor, and those whose rights have been trampled. He faces the evil and finds a way to destroy it. [4]

How do we guard the heart from the toxic effect of exposure to evil?

In "The relevance of spirituality in policing: a dual analysis," Jonathan Smith and Ginger Charles relate research that indicates that every day in America one police officer reaches the point where he feels his life no longer has meaning, and he tragically kills himself. [5]

They go on to point out that their research has revealed clear evidence that spiritual practices can help police officers cope with the toxic nature of their job. [6]

For Smith and Charles it was clearly just as important to ask whether the human inside the uniform has the connection, compassion, and inner strength to meet human destruction and suffering, see his or her way to the other side, and remain whole in the process. [7]

These researchers rightly see spirituality as the way to remain whole when dealing with the toxic effects of exposure to evil. However, is there a way officers so exposed can flourish and reach a level of self-actualization in policing that can be a force for good that transforms society?

What type of spirituality would allow you to move beyond survival and into a world where every day was a day of opportunities that allows the power of compassion, peace, and hope to permeate your consciousness and impact your world?

How do we achieve inner armor, happiness, tranquility, peace, harmony, and balance so that our outer world of action draws on the law of attraction?

When mind, body, spirit, and soul are at peace, the opportunities to serve are always present.

For Dr. Joseph Murphy, in *The Power of your Subconscious Mind*, it is wisdom that gives you an awareness of the tremendous spiritual powers in your subconscious mind and the knowledge of how to apply these powers to lead a full and happy life. [8]

Despite being persecuted and a refugee from his own country, the Dalai Lama says that according to his own experience, the highest level of inner calm comes from the development of love and compassion. [9]

For him true compassion is impartial and bears with it a feeling of responsibility for the welfare and happiness of others. [10]

Marcus Aurelius wrote, "He who lives in harmony with himself lives in harmony with the universe."

The Buddha, who searched for wisdom his whole life, taught, "Just as treasures are uncovered from the earth, so virtue appears from good deeds, and wisdom appears from a pure and peaceful mind. To walk safely through the maze of human life, one needs the light of wisdom and the guidance of virtue."

How do we explore and appropriate the type of spiritual wisdom that will give us interior peace and harmony?

For Special Agent Samuel Feemster, of the FBI Behavioral Science Unit, spirituality does not weaken the best aspects of policing; rather, it greatly accentuates them. [11]

Feemster relates that at the first annual *Beyond Survival: Wellness Practices for Wounded Warriors Conference* held at the FBI Academy, the conference findings revealed seven ways in which spirituality matters in law enforcement:

1. Spirituality nourishes the inner being of officers, inoculating, protecting, and refreshing them from dangerous levels of multiple stressors.

2. Spirituality unleashes vitality for reengaging officers in the spirit of the law.

3. Spirituality heals the deepest, most invisible trauma of wounded warriors.

4. Spirituality provides an antidote for the toxicity of evil, thereby promoting wellness beyond survival.

5. Spirituality nurtures longevity in law enforcement.

6. Spirituality enhances intuitive policing, emotional intelligence, and stress management.

7. Spirituality, according to new evidence, strengthens brain functions. [12]

Those who seek wisdom will find it. Those who scoff at the notion that the experience of the sages of history can help them are also right. If you think you can do it, you're right. If you think you can't do it, you're also right.

Wisdom is the pearl of great price, and is the prize to be sought above all else. In wisdom we have the ability to develop a spirituality that informs everything we do and that leaves a lasting legacy of peace as we actualize it in our lives.

From the heart love can flourish if you want it to. Evil will be repelled in your inner person and your outer actions, if you want it to. You can *tap in* to a developed inner spirituality, or you can *tap out* of a search for inner peace and harmony.

Your decision will impact the world.

ENDNOTES:

1. Dalai Lama, *My Spiritual Journey*, collected by Sofia Stril-Rever (New York, NY, Paris, France: HarperOne and Presses de la Renaissance, 2009-2010), p.1.

2. Michael Dye, *The Peacekeepers, A Bible Study for Law Enforcement Officers* (Longwood, Florida: Advantage Books, 2005), pp.20-21.

3. Ken Sande, *The Peacemaker, A Biblical Guide to Resolving Personal Conflict* (Grand Rapids, Michigan: Baker Books, 1991, 1997), p.64.

4. Kevin McInnes, *The Servant Warrior, The Role of Faith in Policing* (Calgary, Alberta: Off Duty Partners For Life, 2008), p.50.

5. Jonathan Smith and Ginger Charles, "The relevance of spirituality in policing: a dual analysis" (*International Journal of Police Science & Management*, Volume 12, Number 3), p. 321.

6. Ibid, p.333.

7. Ibid, p. 336.

8. Joseph Murphy, PhD, *The Power of Your Subconscious Mind* (Toronto, New York, Sydney, Auckland: Bantam Books, 1963), p.213.

9. Dalai Lama, *My Spiritual Journey*, p. 26.

10. Ibid, p. 20.

11. Samuel L. Feemster, First Annual *Beyond Survival: Wellness Practices for Wounded Warrior Conference* (Quantico, VA:

FBI Law Enforcement Bulletin, May 2009, Volume 78, Number 5), p. 3.

12. Ibid, pp. 3-4.

CHAPTER 9

Not Talk, But Action—Non Loqui Sed Facere

~Evil triumphs when good men do nothing.

Sir Edmund Burke~

J oey LaMatta, the day manager of the Ambassador Hotel, was pissed. Even the hookers who used the hotel for hot sheets, complained about the couple screaming at each other in room 204.

Joey decided to phone the cops when he heard a woman in that room screaming, "Don't kill me!"

Officer Bob Arnett responded to room 204 and found a sergeant and two other cops from the downtown division discussing what to do. They could all hear the woman screaming at the top of her lungs for someone not to kill her.

Bob couldn't understand why everyone was having this discussion. It wasn't his call, as he was the third unit out. There was a sergeant on scene who should have been taking control, but that didn't seem to be happening.

Bob kicked the door in. As he entered the small room, a ratty brown bathrobe on a hook behind the door, wrapped around his head. Bob glimpsed a large butcher knife in a man's hand on the down-stroke towards a female under him on the bed.

Bob grabbed the knife hand and twisted the knife away from the woman, who was still screaming hysterically. The other officers helped handcuff the male, who was still struggling to get at the woman.

The cops found out that the couple were married and both high on cocaine. The woman turned on them and began yelling obscenities.

It was hard to believe. By a split second, Bob had literally saved her from being stabbed in the heart, and here she was cursing them with every breath. The tiny, dismal room was full of drug paraphernalia and a few grams of cocaine.

The sergeant directed the initial car crew to take the man and the woman to jail.

The knife had caused a small cut to the web of Bob's right hand when he went to grab it, and he headed off to the ER to get a tetanus shot.

His take was that talk when action was required was stupid. A split second more hesitation and they would have been investigating a homicide. It didn't look like there was much appreciation from the citizen they had saved, either. Bob could chalk that up to the devil-cocaine.

The non-action of his fellow officers bothered him. When the sergeant made sure they all got a commendation letter for their heroic efforts, he threw his in the garbage.

~Maintain the right

Royal Canadian Mounted Police Motto~

Recently two young police officers were overheard talking in a booth at a diner about limiting liability. They felt that today in policing you had to watch out for number one.

Why expose yourself to criminal and civil liability when all you had to do was be politically correct, take only the calls assigned, and just clean up the inevitable messes people leave in their wake?

Make sure you've done your paperwork prior to end of shift, and if you don't investigate too hard you won't be bothered with going to court on your days off.

In essence, you needed to keep fit and avoid toxic stress so you didn't die ten years earlier than the rest of society.

It makes sense doesn't it? The public doesn't want the police to arrest anyone, and any cop that does, gets his ass handed to him internally, in the press, in the courts, and with his liberal live-in girlfriend.

The gopher that sticks his head out of the hole gets it shot off. Why bother? No one cares! Do the time and get a pension. You just need to navigate through the potholes.

~Semper fidelis—Always faithful

Motto of the US Marine Corps~

Of course, not all police officers think this way. Thank God!

The problem we have today is that some young officers do feel this way. Increasingly, people are not even phoning the police about crimes or disturbances because their interactions with the police have led them to conclude that no investigation is going to be conducted anyways. So why bother?

Police leaders pat themselves on the back and tell the public that crime has gone down and they have the statistics to prove it. Of course, you know what they say about how statistics are manipulated.

The reality is that public confidence in the police has gone down dramatically in the past two decades. Cynical cops with an arrogant attitude have led to an "us" against "them" perspective for both the police and the public they are supposed to serve.

Peacemaking is on the wane, and report-taking clerks who call themselves police officers are on the rise. Police have begun to lose sight of their sacred calling to serve. Many have been unfaithful to their oath of office, and its no big deal to them.

The questions the public asks are: "What happened?" "Where have our honorable and brave guardians gone?" "Why don't our police want to go into harm's way to protect us anymore?" "Why don't they investigate crime anymore?" "Why does it seem like the police want us to serve them and not the other way around?"

Is it a leadership issue? Are formal and informal leaders with nobility, integrity, honor, courage, and virtue becoming a rarity now?

Martin Luther King Jr. said, "A nation or civilization that continues to produce soft-minded men purchases its own spiritual death on the installment plan."

For Marcus Aurelius; "A noble man compares and estimates himself by an idea which is higher than himself; and a mean man, by one lower than himself. The one produces aspiration; the other ambition, which is the way a vulgar man aspires."

Len Marrella, in *In Search of Ethics* tells us that from honest and ethical conduct comes trustworthiness; from trustworthiness comes respect; and when we respect each other we are fair and just. This is the key to peaceful and harmonious, productive relations. [1]

In the past the public expected the police to pay full-time attention to the duties incumbent on every citizen, as expressed so well in the past by Sir Robert Peel, the acknowledged founder of modern policing methods.

Today we have a trust issue. If police officers do not serve people with integrity, and right character, the public trust will continue to erode until the privilege to serve is withdrawn from the police.

Anarchy lurks in the weeds when the police refuse to do their jobs. Every time an officer refuses to do his sworn duty, a crack in the body politic emerges.

Core values of police departments are only a useless piece of paper on the wall unless the core values are an integral part of the inner personhood of police officers. Only an integrated, moral worldview that necessarily exposes itself in right thinking, right action, and peacemaking will turn the tide of current public dissatisfaction.

A police officer's willingness to be a natural leader because of an inner spirituality that embraces wisdom, courage, virtue, and zeal to serve the public, even to the point of death, is the key to a revival of the public trust.

The police leader must also remind the public that many centuries ago Aristotle told us that, "Among good citizens the salvation of the community is the common business of them all." [2]

Of course, if the police leader doesn't have credibility with the public, it will be a hard-sell convincing citizens to be part of the solution to public safety. The climb up this mountain of indifference can seem overwhelming to many police officers unless they embrace Thomas Jefferson's view; "One man with courage is a majority."

How do the police regain the desire to go into harm's way to protect the citizens they serve?

For Captain John Paul Jones, of the American Navy of 1747-1792, it was a resolve and a, "wish to have no connection with any ship that does not sail fast, for I intend to go into harm's way."

Captain Jones understood his duty and relished the call to serve. Going into *harm's way* was his job and he was prepared for the challenge.

Like any change for the better, it starts by looking in the mirror and changing one's own attitudes and behavior. Taking a look inside and being resolute in learning to harness the energy of inner spirituality will be a good first step. Changes within will release the outward expression of action.

It is impossible to be a true peacemaking police officer unless you have inner peace.

For Inez Tuck, PhD, spirituality is the coexisting and transitional state of *being* and *becoming* in relation to the emergent nature of interiority and connectivity. It is through efforts such as self-reflection, meditation, and contemplation, that energy or life force is directed or transformed into manifestations of hope, peace, love, belongingness, generosity, and the inner strength necessary for physical, spiritual, and mental well-being. It creates meaning and purpose in the reality of one's existence, as well as expands potentialities and possibilities. [3]

Talk is cheap.

Action means having an intention that is acted upon. When our actions are guided by mission, purpose, and vocation and are a reflection of courage of convictions arising from an inner spiritual harmony, we will do the right thing, at the right time, and for the right reasons.

ENDNOTES:

1. Len Marcella, *In Search of Ethics* (Sanford, Florida: DC Press, 2009), p. 198.

2. Ibid, p. 209.

3. Inez Tuck, PhD, "On the Edge-Integrating Spirituality into Law Enforcement" (Quantico, VA: *FBI Law Enforcement Bulletin*, May 2009, Volume 78, Number 5), pp. 19-20.

CHAPTER 10

Forewarned is Forearmed—
Praemonitus Praemunitus

~Love is an action verb.~

R ob Anderson loved the east coast with its sandy beaches, friendly people, seafood, and history. Going lobster fishing with his buddy Marty and farming with his father resonated in his soul. Feeling the soil in his hands and helping plants root and grow drew him strongly to the land.

Mary Ening, his girlfriend, was great as well. She was not only lovely, but also friendly, out-going, and loving to her family, friends, and to him. Rob had met her at a church social event and they had been going steady for a year. He liked her family, and they seemed to like him.

But then there was that Sunday in church when he got an interior message, *Break up with her.* He recognized the internal voice that wasn't audible but was spoken to his soul as the same voice that had guided him so often in the past. You knew it wasn't your own imagination because it always asked you to do something you didn't want to do. You couldn't understand the why of it because you didn't have the ability to see the future.

No way! You didn't stop going out with someone you like. Someone you thought about marrying. It didn't make any rational

SPIRITUALITY: INNER ARMOUR

sense. But, every week at church he would hear the same interior voice persist in telling him to break up with Mary. He kept resisting.

Rob knew she would ask him why. What was he going to tell her, "I hear voices"? She would question his sanity, and frankly he was questioning this as well.

Still, Rob knew he would have to break up with Mary, although everything inside him resisted.

The problem he had was that in the past, and especially last summer when he had walked the Appalachian Trail along the east coast, that same interior voice had saved his life, guided him, and protected him in amazing ways.

Rob had decided to take the summer off between his first and second year of college and hike the Appalachian Trail through Massachusetts, Connecticut, New York, and New Jersey. He was going to finish the hike by attending a conference at Princeton, New Jersey, and then make his way back north to get home.

While hiking through New York State, Rob was concerned because he only had fifty-two dollars left to last him the rest of the trip. He was going into a small village the next day just off the trail and knew he would have to spend two dollars and fifty cents for supplies, thus breaking the fifty. He would still have a long way to hike, and then he had to make his way back to college.

That day he hiked twenty miles and then camped beside a flowing stream, set up his tent, and had supper. He was settled in for the night when he heard an interior voice say, *Get up and walk!*

It didn't make sense. He had done his twenty miles and camped beside flowing water where he could wash up and cook. But Rob packed up his tent, picked up his backpack, and walked another mile until he saw a plateau with a grassy field. It felt right and so he pitched his tent, took his Bible and went to a big pine tree and used it as a backrest while he read. When he looked between his legs he saw a silver dollar. Here was the exact amount of money needed to not have to break the fifty for the next two weeks. Coincidence?

Did he trust the inner voice? Had the inner voice ever lied to him in the past? Could he trust that the author of the inner voice knew what he was doing, even if Rob couldn't figure it out now?

Mary couldn't understand why Rob would break up with her. "Don't you like me?"

Rob scrambled for an explanation that wouldn't sound like he'd lost his marbles. "Mary, I think we are both pretty young and we need to mature a bit before we continue going out."

The hurt look she gave him cut him to the core.

Every Sunday at church when Rob saw Mary he had fresh doubts. It still didn't make any sense, and yet, he couldn't resist the message received. There had to be some sense to this, or maybe he was crazy.

College was over and not much work was available in the area. His buddy Andy Cook wanted to go to the West Coast to look for work and that sounded like a good idea too. And besides, Rob would be behind the wheel of his 1966 Pontiac for the trip west.

Rob decided he would create a list of character traits and qualities that he wanted in his future wife and mother of his children. First, he wanted an attractive woman who loved God. He wanted her to have morals and values and love her parents and siblings. Rob wanted her to have friends that loved and valued her, and a good work ethic and occupation that utilized her skill sets, talents, and passion. He wanted a good communicator who genuinely cared about people. He would do his due diligence to see how she related with her family, friends and co-workers, and look for red flags like previous relationships, enemies, and financial concerns. He wanted to do the best job he could in starting a relationship off on the right path. Rob also decided that the right woman for him would also have to be okay with God. He didn't want to go through the same experience he had with Mary.

Andy and Rob headed west in the Pontiac and when Rob stepped on the gas a broken engine mount made the engine go sideways while a broken front seat mount made the seat go backward. The four bald tires on the Pontiac didn't help much, but somehow they didn't blow up or go flat on the trip west.

They decided to stop in and see some friends in a western prairie city before going to the West Coast. Joe, Mac, Harry, and Bob had room in their duplex for Andy and Rob, and they could also line them up with a job. Money was tight and Rob wasn't sure if his Pontiac would be able to go much farther anyways, and so they decided to stay put.

That first night, Louise, Brenda, and Ann showed up at the house. They were part of a young-adults group from the local church and sometimes hung out with the men from the duplex.

Rob knew!

It wasn't love at first sight since he didn't really know what that looked like. When Louise popped her head into the living room to get introduced to Andy and him, the knowledge she was going to be his wife and mother of his children was just there. Rob didn't know her yet, but somehow he just knew.

There was a problem, Houston. Rob's buddy, Andy, and a couple of the other guys at the duplex wanted to go out with Louise. Rob didn't want to have to kill them in their sleep, and they would think he was crazy if he told them he was going to marry Louise after one look.

To make matters even more difficult, the whole group was really like a bunch of friends. How was he going to give Louise a hint that he wanted to change a relationship from friend to girlfriend?

As they settled in over the next year, Rob kept dropping hints and Louise kept laughing them off as a joke. He finally got his chance when he signed her twenty-second birthday card, "Roses are red, violets are blue, you're getting old, you should have been sold."

Pretty corny, but it did the trick. Louise had been unsure if she had been misreading the signals Rob had been giving, and now she knew he was serious. Andy had asked her out while they were all at the roller rink the same day Rob was planning to ask her on a date. Luckily, she said yes to Rob and no to Andy. Homicide wouldn't have looked good on Rob's record when he applied to join the local city police.

Rob had already had a full year to do his due diligence on Louise's character and interactions with family, friends, and co-workers. She came up aces in everything, and they were already best friends who could talk about anything. He knew her career in nursing would expose her to shift work, trauma, and compassion fatigue. Louise would be understanding of the stress inherent in police work because of her own experience.

Rob thought about the differences between men and women. Women, for the most part, gave their hearts to the ones they loved, and yet, many women had discovered to their dismay that the commitment of men was not the same. Men, for the most part, were happy to give their bodies, but would not easily give their hearts in a relationship. Many women would pay serious money to know how to gauge commitment in a man they were interested in.

Being a guy - and pretty motivated himself - Rob figured that if a man was willing to respect his future bride enough, he would show his commitment by not only being monogamous but celibate until marriage. The level of commitment would have to be super high on the guy's part if he was willing to respect his girlfriend and her parents and traditions. The real question would be if he was man enough to persevere despite the desire for sexual intimacy. Would he care for Louise enough, love her enough, and have the strength of character to do the right thing?

Lots of couples engaged in premarital sex, and many lived common-law, but Rob made a commitment to himself first of all, and then to Louise, that he would respect her enough to be celibate until marriage. This was going to be his marriage partner and they would share their lives, bodies, hopes, and dreams together.

Rob and Louise had discovered that they were soul mates. Total intimacy of mind, body, and soul would occur after they committed themselves in marriage before God, family, and the community. They would happily commit to a relationship that was legal, moral, spiritual, and open to life.

Rob had been on the job as a police officer for nine months when he stood in the church Louise had attended her whole life before moving seven hundred miles east to become a nurse. Rob had travelled thousands of miles west to find his soul mate and soon-to-be wife. Gratefulness, love, and joy were his because he had listened to the interior voice he could trust.

~We all seek happiness and want to avoid suffering.

Dalai Lama~

The state of our relationships with others can affect our physical, mental, and spiritual psyches in both positive and negative ways. Our most personal relationships can seriously impact our happiness, resiliency, and future. If we understand that police marriages require a strategy, perseverance, and continual effort, along with fine-tuning, we will be on the right path.

When time is taken to determine what character traits are worth looking for in the person we want to have an intimate relationship with, like the time Rob took with Louise in the story, along with due diligence in looking at their interactions with others, we will have the key to longevity and happiness in a relationship.

Statistics reveal that many police marriages and spousal relationships end in discord and failure. The stresses inherent in policing takes their toll on a spouse who is unprepared and uneducated in the effects of toxic evil on the physical, mental, and spiritual psyche of their police spouse.

One of the questions couples need to ask themselves is whether they married their best friend and soul mate. Is there a resonance in their soul with the one they want to have an intimate relationship with? Are doubts lingering at the corners of their consciousness?

If there are doubts, further investigation and due diligence is needed. When the mind, heart, and spirit are in harmony with pursuing a relationship, peace will be the result.

Education with a desire to succeed in spousal relationships through on-going communication and discovery can lead to an intimate, fulfilling, and enduring life together. Those who are forewarned are able to forearm themselves with the methods and strategies that have been proven to improve resiliency, love, commitment, and joy in their most intimate relationships.

While the divorce rate in North America finally stabilized at about fifty percent in 1980, the percentage of single adults has continued to climb up to the present. It is currently at about thirty percent and still rising, because fewer and fewer people are willing to commit themselves to one partner for life. [1]

In his book, *His Needs, Her Needs,* Willard Harley said that marriage therapists were so busy trying to figure out what made marriages fail that they overlooked what made them succeed. Although poor communication, failure to resolve conflicts, and fighting all contributed to marriage breakups, the urgent need was to find ways to restore love in marriages.

Harley's background as a psychologist taught him that learned associations trigger most of our emotional reactions. Whenever something is presented repeatedly with a physically-induced emotion, it tends to trigger that emotion all by itself. Applying the same principle to the feeling of love, he theorized that love might be nothing more than a learned association. If someone were to be present often enough when feeling particularly good, the person's presence in general might be enough to trigger that good feeling - something we have come to know as the feeling of love.

Harley goes on to say, "I could not have been more correct in my analysis. By encouraging each spouse to try to do whatever it took to make each other happy and avoid doing what made each other unhappy, that feeling of love was restored in the very next couple I counseled." [2]

In *The Five Love Languages*, Gary Chapman says that the desire for romantic love in marriage is deeply rooted in our psychological makeup. Gary believes that we must be willing to learn our spouse's primary love language if we are to be effective communicators of love. [3]

His research shows that seldom do a husband and wife have the same primary emotional love language. Once you identify and learn to speak your spouse's primary love language, you will have discovered the key to a long-lasting, loving marriage. [4]

Chapman quotes Dr. Ross Campbell, a psychiatrist who treats children and adolescents, who says, "Inside every child is an 'emotional tank' waiting to be filled with love. When a child really feels loved, he will develop normally but when the love tank is empty, the child will misbehave." [5]

In marriages, the spouses need to spend active, one-on-one time with their children to *hear* the child's heart and respond with love to the child's *love piggy bank*.

Chapman advocates for relationships having a *Love Bank*. If a couple keeps the love bank topped up, the relationship flourishes. If you're always making withdrawals from the bank, you go bankrupt relationally. If a demanding case or work schedule has you seriously depleting your love bank, you need to have an internal *love bank gauge* that can prompt you to replenish the bank.

Those who continually go into the *red* in their relationships with those closest to them shouldn't be surprised when breakdowns in relationships occur.

Chapman has identified the five primary love languages as #1: Words of Affirmation, #2: Quality Time, #3: Receiving Gifts, #4: Acts of Service, #5: Physical Touch.

The object of love is not getting something you want but doing something for the well-being of the one you love. It is a fact, however, that when we receive affirming words we are far more likely to be motivated to reciprocate. [6]

A central aspect of quality time is togetherness. It does not mean proximity. Togetherness has to do with focused attention. [7]

If your spouse's primary love language is receiving gifts, you can become a proficient gift-giver. In fact, it is one of the easiest love languages to learn.

For acts of service, requests give direction to love, but demands stop the flow of love. [8]

Physical touch can make or break a relationship. It communicates hate or love. If your spouse's primary love language is physical touch, nothing is more important than holding her as she cries. [9]

Chapman directs couples to spend some time writing down what they think is their primary love language. Then he has them list the other four in order of importance.

1. What does your spouse do or fail to do that hurts you most deeply? The opposite of what hurts you most is probably your love language.

2. What have you most often requested of your spouse? The thing you have most often requested is likely the thing that would make you feel most loved.

3. In what way do you regularly express love to your spouse? Your method of expressing love may be an indication that would also make you feel loved. [10]

Those who say, "I told you I loved you when I married you; if I change my mind I'll let you know," probably need to express verbally their love or they will most likely become a negative marriage or relationship statistic.

Early in Dr. Harley's career as a counselor, he often felt dismayed to see people with strong religious and moral commitments become involved in extramarital affairs. When basic needs go unmet, you start thinking; *This isn't right, it isn't fair.* [11]

For Harley, marital conflict is created one of two ways: (1) Couples fail to make each other happy, or (2) couples make each other unhappy. In the first case, couples are frustrated because their needs are not being met. In the second case, they're deliberately hurting each other. The first cause of conflict is failure to care and the second, failure to protect. [12]

Harley believes that often the failure of men and women to meet each other's emotional needs is simply due to ignorance of each other's needs, and not a selfish unwillingness to be considerate. [13]

Couples are encouraged to become aware of each other's needs and learn to meet them. "What could your spouse do for you that would make you the happiest?" Harley classifies most of their responses into ten emotional needs: admiration, affection, conversation, domestic support, family commitment, financial support, honesty and openness, physical attractiveness, recreational companionship, and sexual fulfillment. [14]

A look at the chapter titles of Harley's book, *His Needs, Her Needs*, gives the reader a good indication of the very helpful content:

1. How Affair-Proof is Your Marriage?
2. Why Your Love Bank Never Closes
3. The First Thing She can't do Without – Affection
4. The First Thing He can't do Without – Sexual Fulfillment
5. She Needs Him to Talk to Her – Conversation
6. He Needs Her to be His Playmate – Recreational Companionship
7. She Needs to Trust Him Totally – Honesty and Openness
8. He Needs a Good-looking Wife – An Attractive Spouse
9. She Needs Enough Money to Live Comfortably – Financial Support
10. He Needs Peace and Quiet – Domestic Support
11. She Needs Him to be a Good Father – Family Commitment
12. He Needs Her to be Proud of Him – Admiration
13. How to Survive an Affair
14. From Incompatible to Irresistible [15]

How do the spiritual and mental aspects of our personhood intersect with our relationships with our spouses and other significant people in our lives?

In *The Power of Your Subconscious Mind*, Dr. Joseph Murphy gives us a tremendous amount of assistance in our search for knowledge and wisdom.

Whatever thoughts, beliefs, opinions, theories, or dogmas you write, engrave, or impress on your subconscious mind, you shall experience them as objective manifestation of circumstances, conditions, and events. What you write on the inside, you will experience on the outside. You have two sides to your life; objective and subjective, visible and invisible, thought and its manifestation.

Murphy says that your thought is received by your brain, which is the organ of your conscious, reasoning mind. When your conscious or objective mind accepts the thought completely, it is sent to the solar plexus, called the brain of your mind, where it becomes flesh and is made manifest in your experience.

This is why you are always writing in the book of life, because your thoughts become your experiences. The American essayist, Ralph Waldo Emerson said, "Man is what he thinks all day long."

The reason there is so much chaos and misery in the world today is because people do not understand the interaction of their conscious and subconscious minds. When these two principles work in accord, in concord, in peace, and synchronously together, you will have health, happiness, peace, and joy. There is no sickness or discord when the conscious and subconscious work together harmoniously and peacefully. [16]

In human relations with each other, and especially in our closest personal relationships, we need to cherish the other with positive thoughts and actions. If we project positive and loving thoughts, we communicate our inner desire for unity and peace, Murphy says.

For Murphy whatever is impressed in your subconscious mind is expressed on the screen of space. This same truth was proclaimed by Moses, Isaiah, Jesus, Buddha, Zoroaster, Lao Tzu, and all the illuminated seers of the ages. Whatever you feel as subjectively true, is expressed as conditions, experiences, and events. Whatever you impress upon your subconscious mind, the latter will move heaven and earth to bring it to pass. You must, therefore, impress it with right ideas and constructive thoughts. [17]

How does one keep the flame of love alive in our relationships in the mental and spiritual sphere?

Sigmund Freud, the Austrian founder of psychoanalysis, said that unless a personality has love, it sickens and dies. Love includes understanding, goodwill, and respect for the divinity in the other person. The more love and good will you emanate and exude, the more comes back to you. [18]

One of the keys to healthy marriages and intimate relationships is the desire to assist the one you love to realize their aims and ambitions in life. If you hinder another's dream, ambition, and mission, you crush the genius of the other person, and their energy. This usually results in a severe strain on the relationship because of frustration and barriers to being the best person they can be.

In essence, if these people don't give their partners freedom to express their dreams and hopes into reality, they hamper the other's ability to self-actualize.

Murphy says to give no one in the world the power to deflect you from your goal, your aim in life, which is to express your hidden talents to the world, to serve humanity, and to reveal more and more of God's wisdom, truth, and beauty to all the people of the world. Remain true to your ideal. Know definitely and absolutely that whatever contributes to your peace, happiness, and fulfillment must of necessity bless all people who walk the earth. The harmony of the part is the harmony of the whole, for the whole is in the part, and the part is in the whole. [19]

He goes on to say that your inner speech, representing your silent thoughts and feelings, is experienced in the reactions of others toward you. [20]

Murphy points out that many persons habitually set up mental resistance to the flow of life by accusing and reproaching God for the sin, sickness, and suffering of mankind. Others cast the blame on God for their pains, aches, loss of loved ones, personal tragedies, and accidents. They are angry at God, and they believe He is responsible for their misery.

As long as people entertain such negative concepts about God, they will experience the automatic negative reactions from their subconscious minds. Actually, such people do not know that they are punishing themselves. They must see the truth, find release, and give up all condemnation, resentment, and anger against anyone or any power outside themselves, says Murphy. Otherwise, they cannot go forward into a healthy, happy, or creative activity.

The minute these people entertain a God of Love in their minds and hearts, and when they believe that God is their Loving Father, who watches over them, cares for them, guides them, sustains and strengthens them, this concept and belief about God or the Life-Principle will be accepted in their subconscious minds, and they will find themselves blessed in countless ways. [21]

Murphy says that if you really want peace of mind and inner calm, you will get it. Regardless of how unjustly you have been treated, or how unfair the boss has been, or what a mean scoundrel someone has proven to be, all this makes no difference to you when you awaken your mental and spiritual powers. You know what you want, and you will definitely refuse to let the thieves (thoughts) of hatred, anger, hostility, and ill will rob you of peace, harmony, health, and happiness. You cease to be upset by people, conditions, news, and events by identifying your thoughts immediately with your aim in life. Your aim is peace, health, inspiration, harmony, and abundance. Feel a river of peace flowing through you now. Your thought is the immaterial and invisible power, and you choose to let it bless, inspire, and give you peace. [22]

Fear is man's greatest enemy, he says. It is behind failure, sickness, and bad human relations. Love casts out fear. Love is an emotional attachment to the good things of life. Fall in love with honesty, integrity, justice, good will, and success. Live in the joyous expectancy of the best, and invariably the best will come to you. [23]

Many times in the marriage life of a peace officer the tendency of the officer is to not talk to his spouse about the evil encountered during the shift. The thinking is that it was bad enough for the officer to process, so why take it home and cause problems?

The spouse often feels that the officer is not communicating properly and wants to know how their spouse is *feeling* about the incidents at work. The proper response by the officer should be to talk to his spouse about the feelings aroused by the incidents and not to dwell on the gory details. This allows the spouse an insight into the inner person of their partner and they can maintain communicational intimacy as they journey together as one through the joys and sorrows of life.

In *The 7 Habits of Highly Effective People*, Stephen R. Covey draws a lesson from Victor Frankl, a psychiatrist and a Jew persecuted by the Nazis at a death camp during the Second World War. In the midst of the most degrading circumstances imaginable, Frankl used the human endowment of self-awareness to discover a fundamental principle about the nature of man: Between stimulus and response, man has the freedom to choose.

Within the freedom to choose are those endowments that make us uniquely human. In addition to self-awareness, we have imagination – the ability to create in our minds beyond our present reality. We have conscience – a deep, inner awareness of right and wrong, of the principles that govern our behavior, and a sense of the degree to which our thoughts and actions are in harmony with them. And we have independent will – the ability to act based on our self-awareness, free of all other influences. [24]

Patience, kindness, veracity, humility, good will, peace, harmony, and brotherly love are attributes, qualities, which never grow old. If you continue to generate these qualities here on this plane of life, you will always remain young in spirit. [25]

A dynamic spirituality will be the armor that allows inner harmony, tranquility, peace, and joy to extend into our outer relationships. Like all good things in life it takes dedication, hard work, and perseverance to be successful in relationships.

Those who decide to take the easy road will flounder on the rocky road of life. Those who decide their most intimate relationships are worth the continuous effort required to keep the *love bank* topped up will reap the reward of happiness, joy, and peace in a harmonious interdependent reality.

ENDNOTES:

1. Willard F. Harley Jr., *His Needs, Her Needs: Building an affair-proof marriage*, Preface (Grand Rapids, MI.: Baker Books, 2002), p.9.

2. Ibid, p.12

3. Gary Chapman, *The Five Love Languages: How to Express Heartfelt Commitment to your Mate* (Chicago: Norfield Publishing, 1992, 1995), p.13.

4. Ibid, p.16.

5. Ibid, p.21.

6. Ibid, pp.39-41.

7. Ibid, p.59.

8. Ibid, p.76.

9. Ibid, p.105.

10. Ibid, p.124.

11. Harley, *His Needs, Her Needs*, p.22.

12. Ibid, p.15.

13. Ibid, p.19.

14. Ibid, pp.17-18.

15. Ibid, p.1.

16. Joseph Murphy, PhD, *The Power of Your Subconscious Mind* (Toronto, New York, Sydney, Auckland: Bantam Books, 1963), pp.47-48.

17. Ibid, p.47.

18. Ibid, p.174.

19. Ibid, p.177.

20. Ibid, p.178.

21. Ibid, p.180.

22. Ibid, p.195.

23. Ibid, p.210.

24. Stephen R. Covey, *The 7 Habits of Highly Effective People: Powerful Lessons in Personal Change* (New York, London, Sydney, Tokyo, Singapore: Simon & Schuster, 1990), p.69.

25. Murphy, *The Power of Your Subconscious Mind*, p.212.

CHAPTER 11

Kill, or be Killed—Aut Neca Aut Necare

*~My son, when you come to serve the Lord prepare
yourself for trials. Be sincere of heart and steadfast,
undisturbed in times of adversity. Cling to him,
forsake him not; thus will your future be great. Accept
whatever befalls you, in crushing misfortune be
patient; for in fire gold is tested, and worthy men in
the crucible of humiliation. Trust God and he will help
you; make straight your ways and hope in him.*

Sirach 2: 1-6 NAB~

The car-prowling suspects had fled the scene by the time
police arrived. Sergeant Tony Lang had officers circulating the area looking for the two men based on the
description provided by a witness. A canine unit was in the area
and the police helicopter had also shown up to give a visual aerial
platform. No doubt the two bad guys had been casing a vehicle to
steal it until the cops showed up, thought Tony.

He caught a glimpse of two guys headed in the opposite direction from him and swung his police vehicle around to get a better
eyeball. Bingo! The description fit the two suspects and Tony
called in his position. The helicopter put the night-sun spotlight

on the two men. One of the men in front of the police vehicle was visible for a short time and then disappeared from sight when the spotlight moved away.

Suddenly Tony's driver's-side door was pulled partially open and Tony tried to hold it closed while he assessed a deteriorating tactical situation. He looked out the open side window and into the muzzle of a shotgun pointed at his head.

O my God, he was going to die!

Then Tony heard a clear internal voice say, *No, you're not!*

He argued with the inner voice, *Yes, I am going to die!*

He again heard, *No, you're not!*

Tony had always believed that his guardian angel was the big guy, St. Michael the Archangel, the patron saint of police.

From his seated position, he drew and fired his service weapon into the face of the shotgun-wielding man, who immediately went down to the ground. The other startled culprit standing nearby immediately raised his arms and dropped to his knees. The canine unit swung by and helped to handcuff that guy, while an ambulance was called to deal with the badly injured man.

In time, the shotgun-wielding man recovered from his injuries, but Tony was left to deal with the aftermath of the physical, mental, and spiritual trauma. They called it CISM, Critical Incident Stress Management, which was a method of dealing with critical incidents. Tony knew some of this stuff from various training he'd had with peer support, but he also knew that multiple critical incidents could lead to the straw that broke the camel's back.

It had helped Tony to talk to Father Kevin right after the incident. It was also mandatory to talk to a staff psychologist after a shooting, righteous or not, and he was okay with that. He reflected on the Officer Combat Training course he had taken only six weeks earlier. The fact that he had been asked to take the limited-entry course by the trainer was interesting in both timing, and content. The course-attendees had been taught to discharge their weapons while in a seated position in a deadly force-encounter, through both the front windshield and side windows. It was this course that had given Tony the confidence to shoot from a seated position at the bad guy pointing a shotgun at his head.

The reality was that his spirituality and belief in God, seemed to be the only thread that kept him handling the stress professionally and in his personal life.

A previous shooting of a mentally deranged man who'd been knifing his mother-in-law to death in front of a couple of officers didn't help matters. You always have a tendency to second-guess yourself. Should they have shot him sooner before the fatal stab? What could they have done differently? *Why did he make us kill him? Why me?* Guilt, anger, distress and, maybe a case of despair had crept into his life. Dr. Strauss, the shrink he was seeing, had diagnosed him with PTSD; post-traumatic stress disorder.

Tony remembered Father Kevin encouraging him to read a passage from Psalm 34: "The angel of the Lord is encamped around those who revere him, to rescue them. Taste and see that the Lord is good. He is happy who seeks refuge in him." He had felt the presence of his guardian angel at a critical moment and knew the reality of being rescued from death. Despite the ongoing struggles, he had a lifeline to hold onto.

Dr. Strauss had felt that Tony's spirituality had been helpful in trying to deal with his condition. Tony knew he was struggling just to keep his head above water for the most part, but that he felt the healing power of internal peace on occasion at Mass, or when saying the rosary. He was a hurting unit, but at least he wasn't thinking about taking his own life all the time. He hoped that he could be normal one day.

Whatever that looked like.

~I am for peace and they are for war.

Psalm 120:7 NAB~

For those who serve and protect, the reality is that they will meet persons who prefer war to peace. Those who seek war have goals that take precedence over anyone else in society. Being the guardians of society requires a steadfast focus on the vocation, mission, and purpose of peacemaking, despite tribulations. Trials and tribulations can be managed when we can draw on inner spiritual strength that is replenished daily.

Toxic exposure to evil can turn a heart to stone if you allow compassion to die within. A common method of dealing with trauma is to try to contain the emotional impact by compartmentalization. Police try to stuff the impact of trauma into various mental boxes in the hope of being able to deal with a situation in a professional manner. They justify this method by arguing that they have a responsibility to re-establish control, bring order to chaos, and manage evidence, victims, witnesses, and criminals.

Toxic exposure to evil has the potential to bring with it a personal toxic response that includes cynicism, relational impediments, lack of empathy, disassociation from anyone not involved in the same profession, and a distancing from familiar religious practices and spirituality.

A spirituality that breathes life and vitality into the inner person is the key to a life well lived.

What can bring inner harmony and peace to your soul?

Responses to stress, such as compassion fatigue, spiritual distress, and post-traumatic stress disorder (PTSD), have emerged over the past decade as major health issues. [1]

If not appropriately managed, this stress can cause the development of symptoms of PTSD; reactive personality change and substance abuse; physical illness and other co-morbid conditions; and secondary life problems, including relationship breakdowns. [2]

In his report, *Brain Functioning as the Ground for Spiritual Experiences and Ethical Behavior,* Dr. Travis states that he believes spiritual experiences enliven frontal coherence, which builds global circuits to place individual experiences in a larger framework. In this vein, spiritual experiences can provide the inner armor to protect law enforcement officers from the noxious effects of negative experiences and stress. [3]

The concept of spiritual experiences providing inner armor to protect officers is intriguing and hence a part of the title of this book. All of my own experiences, and those which I have observed in many years in service, have led me to firmly believe that spirituality creates an inner armor that protects officers. It's why I chose to title this book with the concept.

Spiritual experiences are a natural outcome of developing our spirituality through openness and a quest for wisdom. Allowing self-actualization, included among Abraham Maslow's *hierarchy of needs,* to empower our actions will give us the inner armor needed to fight the toxic effects of stress.

For Dr. Travis, a higher frontal coherence is correlated with higher moral reasoning, greater emotional stability, and decreased anxiety. [4]

Nelson Mandela, who had spent decades in a South African jail before being released and becoming the president of South Africa, often alluded to William Ernest Henley's poem, *Invictus,* "I am the master of my fate, I am the captain of my soul." Mandela's spirituality buoyed him when he was depressed and felt defeated. His spirituality helped chart a course of reconciliation in the racially charged country when he was elected president. Mandela's inner peace and tranquility allowed him to be the wise and compassionate leader South Africa needed at that critical post-apartheid time.

Police officers today need to emulate the courage and compassion of people like Nelson Mandela. Here was a man jailed for decades who could have succumbed to bitterness, hatred, cynicism, apathy, and despair, yet protected by his inner armor of spirituality emerged with hope, happiness, joy, forgiveness, and peace.

Many people in South Africa and around the world were shocked when Mandela emerged from prison and advocated reconciliation, forgiveness, and peace for all the citizens of his country. Because of his vision and moral authority, he became a societal game changer of the highest caliber.

In our modern world of mediocrity, people are crying out for heroes who are willing to embrace the grand and noble vision of serving and protecting all members of society from the predators who promote evil.

Police officers with a dynamic spirituality, that is constantly replenished with hope, can serve with nobility of purpose and amidst trials see opportunities to be the peacemakers that change the world.

ENDNOTES:

1. Inez Tuck, PhD, "Integrating Spirituality into Law Enforcement" (Quantico, VA: *FBI Law Enforcement Bulletin*, May 2009, Volume 78, Number 5), p. 15.

2. J. Boscarino, "Post-Traumatic stress and associated disorders among Vietnam Veterans" (Quantico, VA: *FBI Law Enforcement Bulletin*, May 2009, Volume 78, Number 5), p. 18.

3. Fred Travis, PhD, "Brain Functioning as the Ground for Spiritual Experiences and Ethical Behavior" (Quantico, VA: *FBI Law Enforcement Bulletin*, May 2009, Volume 78, Number 5), p. 31.

4. Ibid. p. 31.

CHAPTER 12

Deeds, not Words—Acta Non Verba

*~The difference between what we do and what we are capable
of doing would suffice to solve most of the world's problems.*

Mahatma Gandhi~

S tu was driving west towards his home after the evening
shift and was in awe of the huge harvest moon that illuminated the sky when he heard that familiar interior voice
say, *You call yourself pro-life. How about you put your words into
action and start a maternity home for pregnant teenage girls with no
place to go, who resort to abortion out of desperation?*

Wow! That inner voice had to be God. It sure wasn't part of
Stu's thinking. Spending forty to fifty hours a week building his
dream log house in the country while working full time as a cop
didn't leave a lot of time for other activities. What with court
appearances on days off, being a deacon in his church, and being
an uncle-at-large for a troubled teenager, there just wasn't much
time for other stuff. Oh, yeah! Throw in marriage and four kids.
Stu didn't mean to say that marriage and kids were his last priority, they were his first. Marrying his dynamo soul mate had made
life more enriching than even his wildest dreams envisioned. Stu
took to heart that saying, "If the wife is happy, everyone is happy."

Where was he going to get the time to do this? Was there even a need for a maternity home? Who was going to pay for it? Why him?

Sarah, his wife, thought it was a great idea. How many maternity homes were there in the city?

Great question.

The next day, Stu broached the subject with Kevin, his Catholic crime-fighting partner. Kevin and his wife, Teri had been involved in the pro-life movement for years and they also wondered how many maternity homes there were in the city. For a city approaching a million citizens you would think there would be lots of safe homes for pregnant teens.

On coffee break, Stu and Kevin tracked down the director of the local crisis pregnancy center and asked her if there was a need for a maternity home in the city.

"We've been praying for three years for someone to come through the door and ask us that question." She went on to explain that the Salvation Army had closed its ten-bed maternity home three years earlier because of a lack of funding and they had found it difficult to house pregnant girls in crisis in private homes. They had one young, pregnant client whom they had put in a social-service youth-crisis home, and she had been kicked down some stairs by another girl and had subsequently lost her baby.

It was shocking to think that no safe and secure housing was available for vulnerable, pregnant teenagers in the whole city. Stu knew that the message from God to do something was real. He threw up a challenge prayer request. "Lord, if you want this maternity home to house your needy children, I will be a catalyst. You know how busy I am, so I need you to make this happen."

Ok, what to do? It just so *happened* that the very next day there was a church board meeting with the pastor, elders, and deacons. The agenda dealt with selling the parsonage the pastor no longer lived in, and using the proceeds to pay down the debt on the church.

The clerk of the board agreed to allow Stu to speak to the issue of the parsonage before general discussion began.

Stu was a bit nervous, but knew he had a responsibility to begin the journey.

"Brothers, I believe the Lord is calling us to not only say we are pro-life but to demonstrate our love for those in need by opening a maternity home for unwed mothers here in the city. I would like to use the parsonage as a maternity home to put our beliefs into action. Currently there are no maternity homes in the city, and according to the crisis pregnancy center there is a desperate need for one."

Stu knew that everyone there was aware of the pregnancy center since at least once a year they'd had a collection for that organization, but there was complete silence from the fifteen men around the table. Had he blown it?

The chairman of the board cleared his throat and said, "Great idea. Let's take a vote on this proposal. All in favor say aye, those opposed say nay."

It was unanimous to go ahead with the proposal. In the silence, the Holy Spirit had been gently stirring hearts to be compassionate to these little ones in need.

Stu was to form a committee; renovate the parsonage to accommodate house parents; organize volunteers; obtain furniture; prepare a budget; do fund raising; build protocols; develop a working relationship with the pregnancy crisis center and other social agencies for counseling for the girls, vet and hire staff, and perform a myriad of other duties he was not yet aware of.

What a ride. The committee came together right away. Stu's wife, his police partner Kevin, and others from the church joined and were given various tasks. An army captain, moving back to the barracks at the base donated his entire household contents. A contractor at the church volunteered to do the house-parent suite renovation at material cost. It would cost about five thousand dollars in materials.

Parishioners donated money and volunteered to help the pregnant teens get to medical appointments and counseling sessions, and to mentor them with skills in baby care, finances, and life. A couple with two children felt God calling them to be house parents, although they felt sure they were disqualified because they had children and there might not be enough room. After an interview it was clear that they were the ones to be the compassionate hands and hearts to comfort, guide, and support these vulnerable, pregnant girls.

~

It had been a busy night for the police. At one o'clock in the morning Stu and Kevin responded to a call of an unwanted guest. The basement they investigated had bare stud walls with junk in the corners, a smell of despair, and a frightened, fourteen-year-old, pregnant girl.

She didn't want to work the streets anymore, and was visibly pregnant. Tears left trails on her face as she looked at them in desperation. "I've got nowhere to go. I've tried couch-surfing, but no one wants me anymore. My parents kicked me out and now my friends want me out. I got beat up last time I went to the shelter and don't want to go there."

Her tears battered Stu's heart. "It just so happens that I can bring you to a safe maternity home where they will feed and take care of you. You can have your own room and have a safe place to be for you and your baby. Would you like us to take you there?"

This fourteen-year-old became the first resident in the maternity home God helped Stu and his friends to open several days later.

At its grand opening, the maternity home welcomed its first three pregnant teens. The home had been nine months in the making. God has a sense of humor.

~He who knows when he can fight,
and when he cannot, will be victorious.

Sun Tzu, *The Art of War~*

Spirituality develops a capacity to hear the voice of God. Whether for you God is a higher being or a concept, our ability to hear with an inner ear can be developed through meditation, prayer, education, and stillness. But to develop inner armor, tranquility, centeredness, and peace, there must be a desire for harmony in the inner and the outer person.

The Dalai Lama states, "According to my own experience, the highest level of inner calm comes from the development of love and compassion." [1] He goes on to say, "True compassion is impartial and bears with it a feeling of responsibility for the welfare and happiness of others." [2]

Deeds, and not just words or philosophy, should be the guiding light of an inner spirituality that is enveloped by compassion for the human condition in one-self, and for the other in need. Being open to the power of love allows one to be compassionate, and compassion in action is the road to happiness.

Being open interiorly to works of mercy allows one to serve others with sincerity and authenticity. True service requires humility.

In *The Servant,* James C. Hunter describes humility as "Not thinking less of yourself, it's thinking about yourself less." [3]

A spirituality that allows you to be responsive to the needs of others will also lessen the toxic effects of evil, because tribulation, temptation, and despair will be reframed within the context of opportunity to meet a need that only you can respond to-or *not* respond to. We all have the ability to make choices.

The challenge in life is about the choices we make when presented with dilemmas in our own lives and the lives of those we serve. An active, informed spirituality allows one to see an opportunity and then respond in service and love. Spirituality that is integrated into a harmonic inner congruence will be compelled to act with deeds when words won't suffice for those in need.

~

The maternity home was meeting the needs of the young, pregnant residents, and there had been interest from other churches to help support and maybe replicate the model to meet the growing needs for crisis housing. The present maternity home could handle only three young women at a time due to various regulatory issues.

Stu and Kevin were invited to have a booth to promote the ministry for pro-life Sunday at a large evangelical church in the city's northwest. They had never been in this particular church and marveled at the large, theatre-like auditorium. They decided to sit in on the service and enjoyed the sermon, singing, and worship. On this Sunday, the church had adult baptism in a large hot-tub-size baptismal font for full immersion. One of the men baptized dried off and then came to the pulpit to give his testimony.

The man related that he had been a drug enforcer. He and his partner had gone around beating people for unpaid drug debts. But now, he had found the Lord and was a changed man. He wanted to commit his life in service to God.

Stu and Kevin looked at each other. The man looked a lot like a guy who had escaped them. Stu's mind went back to that traumatic experience a year previous.

The call had come in as a disturbance at a house. Stu and Kevin weren't too hyped about it, as these calls were pretty regular. The two badly beaten men in the back yard were unusual, though. They indicated that the two men who had beaten them up were currently inside their house stealing stuff. Kevin called for backup, and Stu went in first through the back door and up the three steps that led into the kitchen.

Just as Stu was about to yell "Police!" he found a handgun pointed at his face. The guy had the drop on him, and Stu immediately backed down the steps and yelled, "Gun!" to Kevin. Stu saw the man throw the handgun behind the couch and run for the front door. Another man also ran for the front door in his bid to escape.

The call for backup was a partial success. A car crew was able to arrest the brawny culprit running south on the street in front of the house. They took him down hard and after handcuffing him, discovered a large butcher knife with a wide blade in his belt, hidden against his back under his clothing. The other man had run north on the street and escaped before the scene was contained. Stu had gotten a look at him when he was in the hall and the description went out to circulating units without success.

From behind the couch, Stu recovered the .357 caliper Smith & Wesson handgun with six live rounds for evidence. The officers determined from the story they got from the beaten men that the men had owed a drug debt, and that the two enforcers had come to collect a pound or two of flesh and any other valuables they could find in the home.

Drug dealers who had been beaten by drug debt collectors. Go figure.

The suspect who had pointed the handgun at Stu was interviewed at the station. At 250 lbs. and six feet tall, he was a muscled and large man. He readily admitted that he and a partner, had come to collect on a drug debt and had beaten the two drug dealers. He said he initially thought that the police were bikers coming to take them out, and he indicated that if Stu had had a weapon in his hand he would have shot him. When the culprit realized Stu and Kevin were the police he had tossed the gun, run out the door, and gotten caught. He declined to name his accomplice.

Stu was not happy! Having a gun pointed at you from a foot away is what they call a "critical incident." Although Stu knew rationally that he had not been shot because he had not had a gun in his hand, he resolved to never allow anyone to get the drop on him again. He made up his mind that he would draw and fire at anyone who pointed a firearm at him, and take his chances.

Stu did a ballistic test on the handgun at the range and sure enough it fired a round nicely. The beaten-up drug dealers refused to show up in court and the break and enter and assault charges were dropped. The judge felt that pointing a firearm at a police officer in the execution of his duties was only worth a six-hundred dollar fine. Stu was tempted to share the experience with the judge to demonstrate the fallacy of that assumption.

Six months after the incident, a classmate of Stu's from recruit class had been shot in the head by a drug-dealing ex-cop from Barbados. Stu was asked to be a pallbearer and attended the full-honors police funeral.

The father of the slain cop was a retired police member, and although he showed a lot of courage, you knew that he had never expected to outlast his son.

At the liquid wake in the police bar, with cops from across North America, Stu flashed back to his own critical incident involving a gun and tried desperately to allow the drink to drown out the pain. Luckily, a sober, uniformed buddy drove him to his country home.

Yes, Stu's spirituality helped him manage the incident, but having a loving and understanding wife, friends, and faith helped a lot, as well.

And here they were now. A reformed drug enforcer had found the Lord. Should Stu follow an impulse and arrest him right off the pulpit, or could he rejoice that the prodigal son had returned home? Did he see the face of Jesus in everyone he met, as Mother Theresa put it, or did he just see the face of a criminal?

Stu and Kevin looked wryly at each other. After all, the drug dealers hadn't wanted to pursue assault charges and this former drug enforcer had turned his life around. The partners were both thinking the same thing. There but for the grace of God, go I.

~

To forgive is to give something for. Give love, peace, joy, wisdom, and all the blessings of life to the other, until there is no sting left in your mind. This is really the acid test of forgiveness. [4]

ENDNOTES:

1. Dalai Lama, *My Spiritual Journey*, collected by Sofia Stril-Rever (New York, N.Y., Paris, France: HarperOne, Presses de la Renaissance, 2009,2010), p.26

2. Ibid, p.20

3. James C. Hunter, *The Servant* (New York: Crown Business, Random House Inc., 1998, 2002), p.111.

4. Dr. Joseph Murphy, *The Power of the Subconscious Mind* (Toronto, New York, London, Sydney, Auckland: Bantam Books, 1963), p.189.

CHAPTER 13

Spiritual Armor—Spiritualibus Armis

*~Man learns through experience, and the spiritual path is
full of different kinds of experiences. He will encounter many
difficulties and obstacles, and the very experience he needs to
encourage and complete the cleansing process.*

Sai Baba~

The 911 call came in from a motorist travelling under the bridge. It appeared that a large person was attempting to jump off the bridge onto the roadway.

Officer Geoff Doherty and his partner Gary Turner responded to the call on the outskirts of a small western city. Heavy fog made driving fast difficult but they got there in five minutes. Geoff got out on the bridge deck to check out the call while Gary parked the police vehicle safely on the side of the bridge.

Geoff noticed a large, three-hundred-pound First Nations woman trying to lever herself over the four-foot railing. He went to her immediately and tried to get her to talk. She ignored him and was able to get onto the railing. When Geoff grabbed her, their combined weight started to pull both of them over the railing. He wasn't going to let go.

A large First Nations man came up to Geoff and said, "You look like you need a hand," and they both easily pulled the woman back onto the bridge deck. The man then started walking in the fog toward the other officer. Geoff yelled to his partner to grab the guy's name for the police report.

Gary came up to his partner with a quizzical look on his face and said, "What guy are you talking about?"

"The native guy that was walking towards you. He saved my life as well as this lady's here."

Gary looked at him and said, "There was no guy that walked towards me. The fog wasn't that thick that I wouldn't have seen him."

After getting the woman to ER at the hospital to have a psyche exam, Geoff and Gary went for coffee.

"Geoff, are you sure you saw a native guy?"

"I'm sure. That guy saved my life and that native gal's. I can't figure out where he disappeared to."

When Geoff went to the reserve just south of the city several months later, he decided to talk about the incident to his friend Clay Spotted-Horse, a First Nations elder of the Blackfoot Nation.

"Geoff, that native man that saved your life, and the life of the woman, was your "Watcher!" said Clay.

"Was it the Watcher for the native lady?" asked Geoff.

"It was *your* Watcher!"

"Clay, how is that possible?"

"Geoff, the Great Spirit is in all things and situations. You needed help and I believe that your Watcher appeared in visible form to protect you."

It was hard to argue the presence of a guardian Watcher when he saved your life, Geoff supposed, but who would believe it?

~

There is an old saying that goes like this: "For those who believe no explanations are necessary, and for those who disbelieve no explanations are possible."

In the spiritual realm, mystery is part of the experience. Sometimes events happen in our lives that defy rational explanation.

When police officers put on their outer body armor for protection they also need to check that their inner spiritual armor is in place to deal with the toxic effects of evil. A resilient spirituality can deal with any challenge thrown at it.

Fundamentally, spirituality is related to our personhood. Our persons include our bodies, psyches, and spirits. A person is a being in relationship with other persons, which necessarily includes a personal way of relating to the environment (plant and animals). [1]

In *Understanding Christian Spirituality,* Michael Downey says that in understanding spirituality in general terms today, there is awareness that there are levels of reality not immediately apparent; there is more than meets the eye. Second, there is a quest for personal integration in the face of forces of fragmentation and depersonalization. In Downey's view, those are the two spirituality constants; the two essential components in any approach to spirituality. [2]

He goes on to say that in addition to breeding narcissism and bottom-line pragmatism, the culture in which we live instills in us an unbridled restlessness. We are hungry for experience. We are afraid to be alone. We cannot be still. Put briefly, we need constant excitement and diversion. [3]

The person of deep spirituality must cease running and be still, restful, and receptive to what is. One does not embark on the spiritual way primarily for the purpose of producing certain results or achieving precise outcomes. [4]

A task that awaits us in our common search is to find or make ways of gradually and painfully purging ourselves of the uniquely modern combination of narcissism, restlessness, and above all, bottom-line pragmatism that carry over into the search for the sacred and shape much of the terrain of spirituality today. Until we recognize these three elements as the major problem in spirituality today, we will be at war with ourselves in our quest to live deeply spiritual lives. [5]

When people leave religious institutions because they have been failed or betrayed by them, there is far too often a tendency to think that one can "go it alone" in the spiritual quest. But there remains a need for texts, traditions, and structures of community and authority with which the religious institutions safeguard and serve, albeit sometimes quite poorly. But those who opt out of any religious affiliation are called upon to find other networks of community, tradition, holy writings, and so forth, lest the spiritual quest becomes an individualistic, purely private matter. [6]

For many people today religion has negative connotations. And yet, religion has handed down rich spiritual truths, wisdom, and guidance through the ages. A blanket condemnation of religious texts, traditions, authority, and community ignores the historical reality that in North America and Europe, Christian tradition has shaped our culture, art, literature, and laws, and our institutions like education, health care, social services, and working conditions.

The searcher of wisdom is keen to find the gold nuggets of wisdom that are hidden from those who have a shopping-cart approach to spirituality.

In the *Will of God in Other Words*, Dom Hubert von Zeller gives us some context on the word *religion*, which is derived from the Latin *re-ligo*: I bind back. Practicing religion we bind ourselves back to where we belong. [7]

The Roman Catholic theologian Karl Rahner taught that the spiritual dimension of the person describes the ability human beings possess that enables them to transcend or break out beyond themselves and the limits of self-isolation, self-preoccupation, and self-absorption. This they do through the pursuit of knowledge, freedom, and love. [8]

All human beings are spiritual insofar as all have the capacity to know and be known, to love and be loved, to be free and to enable others to be free. Each one is spiritual insofar as each one is, by nature, drawn to mystery. The different ways of actualizing or realizing these capacities for knowledge, freedom, and love, and the diverse ways of participating in mystery make human beings the very unique and irreplaceable creatures they are. [9]

For Rahner, spirituality refers to the ongoing realization or actualization of the human capacity to move beyond the self in knowledge, freedom, and love, in and through relationship with others and with God. When this self-transcendence is motivated by and directed to relationship with the reality named God, however this is understood, then this spirituality may be said to be specifically religious. But it need not be so. This quest takes on a specifically religious dimension when the person's ultimate concern is God, or when the highest ideal is understood as presence of or union with God. [10]

Different forms of prayer, fasting, almsgiving, and other types of spiritual discipline are expressions of the human desire to surrender completely to unfathomable mystery; to God, who is the source of knowledge, freedom, and love. [11]

The Dalai Lama teaches that he regards every action carried out with good motivation as religious. [12]

He goes on to say that religion implies a system of beliefs based on metaphysical foundations, along with the teachings of dogma, rituals, or prayers. Spirituality, however, corresponds to the development of human qualities such as love, compassion, patience, tolerance, forgiveness, or a sense of responsibility. These inner qualities, which are a source of happiness for oneself and for others, are independent of any religion. That is why the Dalai Lama has sometimes stated that one can do without religion but not without spirituality. And an altruistic motivation is the unifying element of the qualities he defines as spiritual. [13]

For Samuel Feemster, in his article *Spirituality – The DNA of Law Enforcement Practice*, the four basic components of spirituality are:

1. a value-based meaning that emanates from a personal-belief system,

2. the total integration of self in pursuit of holistic meaning,

3. the total integration of self in academic disciplines and vocational service,

4. the recognition of self as a spiritual being on a human journey toward a destiny of that personal-belief system. [14]

Spirit and spirituality have distinct attributes. Spirit depicts an unobservable dimension people must sustain for the same reason that they must nourish their bodies and minds. In contrast, spirituality refers to disciplines undertaken in the care and furtherance of the wholesome or holistic development of the spirit. [15]

Spirituality – a sense of meaning and purpose larger than the instrumental duties of law enforcement – affects the most critical aspects of practice, performance, vitality, and longevity in the profession. [16]

It energizes the ethics of practice, resulting in exemplary (efficient and effective) performance. Whereas performance refers to what tasks officers do to enforce the law, practice is how and why they fulfill their sworn responsibilities, doing so with a spirit that evokes the highest virtues of human dignity (the spirit of the law). Vitality depicts the resilience officers must garner to overcome the toxic evils they encounter in the discharge of their duties. Longevity, which some officers believe encompasses a bar higher than mere survival alone, constitutes the results of nurturing the spirit of the law across many challenges (stresses) and venues of service. [17]

Knowledge can lead to wisdom, but not necessarily. In the spiritual world, wisdom is acquired by those who earnestly seek it. Knowledge that informs and resonates with the soul will be assimilated into our worldview and become an integral inner wisdom we call spiritual intelligence.

Spiritual intelligence in the inner person always seeks to expand its horizons to grow in knowledge of eternal truths and the potential to love without boundaries.

Our purpose here as human beings is to grow toward psychological and spiritual maturity. [18]

Love is not about how you *feel* towards others, but how you *behave* towards others. Love could be defined as the act or acts of extending yourself for others by identifying and meeting their legitimate needs. [19]

This spiritual intelligence can never be fully satisfied, as Buddha found out in his quest for wisdom. To search and to assimilate wisdom is to drink with an unquenchable thirst for the life-giving waters of truth, mercy, and justice.

The natural outflow of spiritual intelligence, properly understood, is an inner tranquility and harmony that allows one the freedom to be still enough to hear the voice of God. Peace in the inner person compels and informs peacemaking in the outer person. Peacemaking begins at home and, like a pebble thrown in a pond, works in us in ever expanding ripples. Peacemaking without inner peace can never fully actualize the potential within.

Spirituality that is powered by compassion and love results in peacemaking actions that are authentic.

In the practice of Ignatian Spirituality, broadly speaking, spirituality describes the way we approach life in terms of our relationship to God. It includes our sense of identity (who we are), vocation (how we are to be and what we are to do), mission (what we are to accomplish), and celebration (how we relate to others and the earth). It includes qualities of our being, such as honor, justice, love, and faith; the way we know ourselves, others, and God; and our communion with others and God. Spirituality embraces the various movements of the spirit that is present within us at all times and draws us to God who is the One, the Beautiful, the True, and the Good.

These movements can come from observing the stars or a beautiful sunset, esteeming the insights of a scholar, or admiring a person dedicated to humanity's well-being. Spirituality takes seriously the inducements and motivations that determine our decisions and actions. [20]

The Dalai Lama calls love and compassion a universal religion. That is his religion. For him compassion, what he sometimes calls human affection, is the determining factor of our lives. [21]

He has gone on to teach that profound happiness, unlike fleeting pleasures, is spiritual by nature. It depends on the happiness of others, and it is based on love and tenderness. [22]

The key to happiness lies in strength of mind, inner serenity, and a quality like steadfastness. [23]

The spiritual revolution the Dalai Lama advocates does not depend on external conditions linked to material progress or technology. It is born from within, motivated by the profound desire to transform oneself in order to become a better human being. [24]

For many police officers and public safety officials, it often feels difficult to keep one's head above water. How do you cope with the demands on time, and of life energy, sapped as if by vampires both on and off the job?

The solution is found within.

By exploring and embracing spirituality in whatever forms resonate with your soul, you will begin to develop a wisdom that informs your spiritual intelligence.

In the *The DNA of Law Enforcement Practice*, Samuel L. Feemster states that intuition is a signal of spirituality just as the sonic boom is a tangible indication that a supersonic aircraft has broken the sound barrier by its excessive speed. Physicists measure light and sound as approximations of unobservable forces at the subatomic level. Intuition senses evil and danger at the hidden level of spirituality in much the same way. Emotion constitutes the coding or interpretation of, or reaction to, the signals provided by spirituality. Ethics refer to the observable habits or behaviors that measure or indicate spirituality and act as a barometer of spiritual wellness. Stress – at alarming rates and in excessive amounts – can activate the breakdown of spirituality. It acts as an ecological virus that precipitates conflicts in ethics, emotions, cognition, and intuition. [25]

Feemster goes on to state that with this in mind, first responders must persistently nurture the core spirituality that informs their attitude, disposition, intelligence, and behavior to remain vigilant, healthy, and effective throughout their chosen vocation. Those either unaware of the spiritual dimension of humanity or not equipped to defend against toxic exposure are overtaken, in varying degrees, by the evil they are called to protect against. [26]

We ignore spirituality at our own peril.

Those who do not realize they are in a war between good and evil will be victims because of unpreparedness. They are defenseless against the toxic exposure to evil and its ill effects on the inner person.

Feemster's article goes on to say that evil can be defined as a destructive, poisonous form of spirituality with outward expressions that degrade, dispirit, disintegrate, dehumanize, and destroy human beings, as well as the set of ideas, dignity, freedoms, networks, property, capital, and activities engulfing the constructive social institutions that people depend on for survival. [27]

The corrosive, cumulative effects of evil upon a spiritually underdeveloped law enforcement officer can prove as deadly as any cancer; heart attack; or chronic, debilitating disease. [28]

Dom Hubert Von Zeller writes that God permits evil while he wills good. God's will should be an invitation, a challenge, to the service of love. [29]

Charity is love in action. How we behave with respect towards others is the action that shows love. Martin Luther King Jr. said, "Love is the only force capable of transforming an enemy into a friend."

For Abbott Blessed Isaac of Stella, charity is the reason why anything should be done or left undone, changed or left unchanged; it is the initial principle and the end to which all things should be directed. Whatever is honestly done out of love and in accordance with love can never be blameworthy. [30]

Create a space that allows you to hear with your interior ear.

Be resolute in searching for knowledge and wisdom because you realize that if you can't get it right in your inner world, you won't get it right in your outer world.

Be willing to hear and share new insights with those closest to you on this journey of discovery.

When you self-actualize wisdom, your spirit will become calmer. Agitation, anger, dissatisfaction, hate, guilt, and fear are expunged from the inner person who has released the toxic effects of narcissism within.

Self-reflection, meditation, forgiveness, confession, prayer, and quiet are some of the practices the masters of spirituality have utilized in their journeys to inner peace.

When you find this inner tranquility, harmony, and peace, the daily ritual of learning, prayer, self-reflection, and gratefulness brings an unlimited well -spring of spiritual fuel to keep you in balance.

When outside influences threaten your spiritual equilibrium, you need to find a quiet space for a time within your physical reality so your inner world can refocus and rebalance.

In the world of policing, tactical decision-making occurs with a dynamic consciousness that your spirituality informs without fear or delay. In inter-personal communication with a spouse, children, coworkers, supervisors, citizens, or criminals, your spirituality animates and directs your listening skills with courage, compassion, mercy, and love.

Critical incidents and the potential toxic effects of evil are mitigated by an awareness of protection and understanding of mission, vocation, and purpose.

A *calling* is defined as "a summons or strong inclination to a particular state or course of action." [31]

A *vocation* is an expression of who and what the person is. If an occupation occupies or captures one, a vocation sets one free to be who that person is called to be. [32]

Vocations ultimately do not take energy *from* us, but give energy and life *to* us. [33]

A policing vocation will involve conflict. Conflict is understood as opportunities to serve. Humility is power under control and allows us the freedom to put away arrogance and narcissistic self-deception.

In Feemster's article, *Spirituality-The DNA of Law Enforcement Practice,* "Spiritual depravity, or dispiritedness, robs officers of discretion, thus rendering them incapable of compassionate and protective enforcement...this hidden terrorism of the spirit shows itself in a lack of concern for spirituality, in a deficient spirituality, and in an unrecognized spirituality. Left unabated, these pernicious indicators pave the road to malpractice in policing via corruption, disrespect, and intolerance. In this damaged state, officers cannot manifest for themselves nor extend to others the spirit of the law (enforcing laws in ways that respect human dignity in other beings)." [34]

The absence of intentional instruction about spirituality (namely, the spirit of the law) inadvertently prevents officers from dealing with the root causes of stress, burnout, despair, cynicism, apathy, suicide, and other maladies associated with toxic exposure to evil. [35]

Several educational steps are needed to protect and serve those who serve and protect.

Feemster goes on to propose that first, the law enforcement profession must begin to appreciate the adverse impact of exposure to evil toxins. Next, it must equip officers to guard proactively against the self-disintegration that can result from exposure to unabated evil. Third, it must develop a curriculum of best practices to be implemented by officers, educators, and communities working together to stem the tide of self-inflicted officer causalities. In addition, law-enforcement training academies must circumspectly collaborate by joining the evolution towards a more holistic curriculum. In conjunction with stress, conflict, crisis management, tactical, and investigative training, as well as physical exercise, an intentional emphasis on spiritual wellness will produce a more effective vocation. [36]

Researchers Jonathan Smith and Ginger Charles also argue that embracing and working with the spiritual dimension needs to be a strategic, organization-wide initiative, where consideration of the spiritual dimension is firmly embedded in the way the organization operates.

This training could also explore and encourage people to consider the toxic effect of policing; the positive and negative coping strategies that can be used by officers; the support mechanisms that are available within the police; and what some of the barriers to accessing these support mechanisms might be.

Their research also highlights the importance of strong relationships, including family, friends, and people outside the police. More information could be provided to family members on support mechanisms available within the police, and on how to access these services. [37]

When we are willing to serve others without barriers, we restore our families, our communities, and our society.

Our spirituality is the only door that allows the potential within us all to flourish in the whole person. We all have the choice to live or die interiorly.

The first step is to seek wisdom. There are no last steps, only growth, for those who seek spiritual enlightenment.

Spirituality is for everyone, but only those who seek will find it.

ENDNOTES:

1. John J. English, SJ., *Spiritual Freedom, From an Experience of the Ignatian Exercises to the Art of Spiritual Guidance* (Chicago: Loyola Press, 1995), p.276.

2. Michael Downey, *Understanding Christian Spirituality* (New York, Mahway, NJ: Paulist Press, 1977),p.14.

3. Ibid, p.19.

4. Ibid, p.20.

5. Ibid, p.21.

6. Ibid, p.22.

7. Dom Hubert Von Zeller, *The Will of God in other Words* (Springfield, IL: Templegate Publishers, 1964), p.25.

8. Downey p.33.

9. Ibid, p.33.

10. Ibid, p.35.

11. Ibid, p. 34.

12. Dalai Lama, *My Spiritual Journey* collected by Sofia Stril-Rever (New York, N.Y., Paris, France: HarperOne and Presses de la Renaissance, 2009,2010), p.83.

13. Ibid, p.105.

14. Samuel L. Feemster, "Spirituality – The DNA of Law Enforcement Practice" (Quantico, VA: *FBI Law Enforcement Bulletin*, November, 2007), p.9.

15. Ibid, p.16.

16. Ibid, p.9

17. Ibid, p.9.

18. James C. Hunter, *The Servant, A Simple Story about the True Essence of Leadership* (New York, NY: Crown Business Random House, 1998, 2002), p.182.

19. Ibid, p.125.

20. English, p.275.

21. Dalai Lama, *My Spiritual Journey*, p.102.

22. Ibid, p. 88.

23. Ibid, p. 89.

24. Ibid, p. 106.

25. Feemster, "Spirituality – The DNA of Law Enforcement Practice," p.11.

26. Ibid, p. 12.

27. Ibid, p. 13.

28. Ibid, p. 13.

29. Von Zeller, *The Will of God In Other Words*, Templegate Publishing, 1964. pp. 8-9.

30. Blessed Isaac of Stella, Abbot, Sermon 31: PL 194, 1292-1293, (New York: Catholic Book Publishing Co., 1975), pp. 195-196.

31. Feemster, "Spirituality – The DNA of Law Enforcement Practice," p.12.

32. Ibid, p.12.

33. Ibid, p.12.

34. Ibid, p.13.

35. Ibid, p.14.

36. Ibid, p. 16.

37. Jonathan Smith and Ginger Charles, "The relevance of spirituality in policing: a dual analysis" (*International Journal of Police Science & Management*, volume 12, Number 3), p.334.

CONCLUSION:

Truth will resonate in your soul. When you explore wisdom and the various paths that persons of influence and game-changers of society have taken in their quests for self-actualization, you will discover common themes that these persons advocate.

For the seekers of wisdom a good place to start is in looking at the wisdom literature of sacred scriptures. Wisdom is always available for the true searcher. "Those who love me I also love, and those who seek me find me." (Proverbs 8:17 NAB)

"The beginning of wisdom is the fear of the LORD and knowledge of the HOLY ONE is understanding." (Proverbs 9:10 NAB)

For police officers who hate evil and seek justice, sacred scripture has this to say: "The fear of the Lord is to hate evil. Pride, arrogance, the evil way and the perverse mouth I hate." (Proverbs 8:13 NAB)

Police officers understand the dictates of duty and justice, and the wealth and treasures of wisdom are available for those who investigate wisdom with diligence. "On the path of duty I walk, along the path of justice, granting wealth to those who love me, and filling their treasuries." (Proverbs 8:20 NAB)

Those who seek an informed spiritual intelligence should pursue the wisdom treasures. We have the opportunity to *tap into* the creative and spiritual energy available to each one of us if we desire to grow in our experience.

Why is this creative and spiritual energy so important to cultivate?

When we allow our creative and spiritual genius to flourish, it brings us energy, vitality, and a desire to *self-actualize*.

When we give ourselves the freedom to *tap into* this energy we also give the freedom and example to our family and friends to express their genius.

In our professional lives this creative and spiritual energy compels us to find solutions or to be part of the solutions to bring hope, dignity, justice, and restoration to the public we serve. This *tapped in* energy sees opportunity in crisis. Serving the despairing and the victims of crime, apathy, and marginalization with humility, courage, kindness, and compassion will be the natural outcome of this creative and spiritual energy.

The following several authors and spiritual giants can help us in our quest to actualize our desire to grow into a holistic person:

William H. Murray has this to say about our creative genius:

"Until one's committed, there is hesitancy, the chance to draw back. Concerning all acts of initiative (and creation), there is one elementary truth, the ignorance of which kills countless ideas and splendid plans: that the moment one definitely commits oneself, then Providence moves too.

All sorts of things occur to help one that would never otherwise have occurred. A whole stream of events issues from the decision, raising in one's favor all manner of unforeseen incidents and meetings and material assistance, which no man could have dreamed would have come his way.

Whatever you can do, or dream you can do, begin it. Boldness has genius, power, and magic in it. Begin it now."

~

In *The Project,* Robin Sharma has also given us a wisdom treasure he wants to shares with us:

"Within each of us lies The Project. An idea longing to be nourished, cherished, launched and completed. Writing a novel. Starting an enterprise. Raising a family. Freeing a nation.

Our deepest desire is to do The Project. To express our vision. To carefully and patiently watch it unfold. To present it to those who will benefit by it. And to experience the pride of a job beautifully done.

Yet, a million distractions battle for our attention. And one hundred doubts fill our hearts. And so slowly and subtly, we recite the excuses that construct our reality. And we shelve The Project. Postponing it for a better day. But postponing The Project is life's greatest lie. Picasso and Basquiat, Einstein and Edison, Jobs and Jay-Z didn't wait for an ideal day to do their dream. They started. When it was hard. Though they had little. While they were alone.

So many of the world's troubles are symptoms of The Project undone. Pain is the result of potential denied. And when you avoid The Project, you dishonor your gifts. Your talents. Your genius. A portion of you goes numb, silent, quiet, scared.

The moment you start The Project, everything shifts. Purpose, focus, passion, and peace return to your life. Eyes sparkle. Energy explodes. Inspiration flows. And your days become supported by coincidence, power, and peak possibility.

This very day, the first of a fresh year - presents your greatest opportunity. To be a lion, not a sheep. To walk with giants versus among the meek. To celebrate your best instead of succumbing to the worst. To lift others up versus to tear others down. To pour creativity, mastery, courage, and light into a world aching for marks of heroism.

So please step up. Release the chains. Dispute all doubts. Start The Project. Do the dream. And change the world. You are responsible for no less."

~

Mother Theresa has wisdom to share which arose out of a spirituality that required perseverance for the long haul of service to the poor and vulnerable of society and she has this to say to us:

"People are often unreasonable, irrational, and self-centered. Forgive them anyway.

If you are kind, people may accuse you of selfish, ulterior motives. Be kind anyway.

If you are successful, you will win some unfaithful friends and some genuine enemies. Succeed anyway.

If you are honest and sincere, people may deceive you. Be honest and sincere anyway.

What you spend years creating, others could destroy overnight. Create anyway.

If you find serenity and happiness, some may be jealous. Be happy anyway.

The good you do today will often be forgotten. Do good anyway.

Give the best you have, and it will never be enough. Give your best anyway.

In the final analysis, it is between you and God. It was never between you and them anyway."

~

Spirituality is our method of internalizing truth, so that it can inform our actions. Each of us has the seed of genius and greatness of soul available to us to explore on this path of life.

Experience can help shape our perceptions, while knowledge points us in the direction of wisdom. Wisdom sought with perseverance will shape our world-view and guide our actions into the path of love. Love is respect for the other that motivates our compassion; our willingness to suffer with the other. Those who serve others on this journey of life will discover the key to happiness.

Jesus, the greatest spiritual master of all time, said about himself, "The Son of Man has not come to be served but to serve – to give his life in ransom for the many." (Mark 10:45 NAB)

Police officers who *tap into* a spirituality that energizes, guides, and guards their souls will not only survive the toxic effects of evil, but will find ways to flourish and grow with the numerous opportunities to serve that will present themselves. A keen awareness and willingness to be available to answer the call will actualize in amazingly profound experiences.

An inner armor of spirituality infused with wisdom will allow the searcher to have calmness amidst the storms of life. This interior harmonic congruence will give tranquility, joy, peace, and serenity, which will be actualized in the outer person in such a way that it will transform society. This congruence is the harmony of the inner and outer person. For those willing to *tap into* the power of mystical spirituality, nothing is impossible.

To ensure your spirituality is tangible, you need to constantly replenish the spiritual fuel to maintain your vocation, mission, and purpose. Those who are willing to discipline themselves for this noble cause will reap the reward of a life well lived.

~

Several centuries ago, John Henry Cardinal Newman shared what he called, *Some Definite Service,* which can inform our vocation, mission, and purpose today:

"God knows me and calls me by name...

God has created me to do some definite service; He has committed some work to me, which He has not committed to another.

I have my mission. I never may know it in this life, but I shall be told it in the next.

Somehow I am necessary for His purposes...I have a part in this great work; I am a link in a chain, a bond of connection between persons.

He has not created me for naught. I shall do good, I shall do His work; I shall be an angel of peace, a preacher of truth in my own place, if I do but keep His commandments and serve Him in my calling.

Therefore I will trust Him. Whatever, wherever I am. I can never be thrown away.

If I am in sickness, my sickness may serve Him; In perplexity, my perplexity may serve Him; If I am in sorrow, my sorrow may serve Him.

My sickness, or perplexity, or sorrow may be necessary causes of some great end, which is quite beyond us.

He does nothing in vain; He may prolong my life, He may shorten it; He knows what He is about.

He may take away my friends, He may throw me among strangers, He may make my spirits sink, hide the future from me – still He knows what He is about...

Let me be Thy blind instrument. I ask not to see – I ask not to know – I ask simply to be used."

~

Each one of us will leave a legacy of some kind to our families and communities. We have a lifetime of choices and decisions that will inform our personal legacies. May our choices reflect our desire to serve with dignity, compassion, perseverance, and right actions.

If police officers, fire, EMS, public servants, and military personnel recognize that they are in a war against the terrorism of evil they will equip themselves, body, mind, and spirit to fight for the righteous and noble calling of peacekeeping. Those who reject the need to equip their whole person, body, mind, and spirit will become victims of the toxic effects of evil.

Our desire to serve with humility, patience, and courage will lead to a life well lived. Only in service to others will we find true happiness. May we hear the words, "Well done, thou good and faithful servant. Enter into my rest."

~

ABOUT THE AUTHOR

Jim Amsing, author of Spirituality: Inner Armor, has over 25 years of experience in law enforcement in both small town and big city policing. Serving as a police chaplain in a major city for 13 years, Jim has dealt with many line of duty deaths and other issues within the police service. Jim has also had extensive training in CISM (Critical Incident Stress Management) and has been involved in many defusing and debriefings. He has also been a crowd control supervisor during G8 and the World Petroleum Congress. Through Jim's passion of seeking to help others, he co-founded Emma maternity House Society; a safe home for pregnant teenage girls who were in a crises housing situation. He also co-founded Legacy Place Society (formally known as Diakonos Peace Officer Retreat Society). This organization was created to develop programs for emergency service and military personnel and families to help deal with the traumatic effects of serving the public by implementing educational programs, as well as emergency housing issues due to medical, post-traumatic stress disorder, and relationship problems. Jim also co-founded the God Squad Canada, a men's yearly workshop on how to be a better father and husband. Jim has been happily married to his soulmate for 40 years, and holds a Bachelors Degree in General studies from St. Mary's University.

Printed in Canada